made in

SASKATCHEWAN

made in SASKATCHEWAN

PETER RUPCHAN
Ukrainian Pioneer and Potter

a biography

JUDITH SILVERTHORNE

REVISED EDITION

SPIRAL COMUNICATIONS INC.

Cover and Book Design: Duncan Campbell
Cover Photo: Saskatchewan Archives Board #A1045 (1),
Peter Rupchan, his workshop, his crafts. Usherville
district ca. 1928. Illustrations: Sinda Shaw/Jeanann Tell
Illustrations are artists' interpretations taken from
available materials.

Canadian Cataloguing in Publication Data

Silverthorne, Judith, date-

Made in Saskatchewan: Peter Rupchan,
Ukrainian pioneer and potter
Includes bibliographical references.

ISBN 0-921435-04-5
1. Rupchan, Peter, 1883-1944. 2. Potters-
Saskatchewan – Biography. 3. Ukrainian Canadians-
Saskatchewan – Biography*. I. Title.

NK4210.R835S551991 738.092 C91-097170-6

Printed in Canada by: Gauvin Press

*This book is dedicated to my husband Alan and son Aaron
for their loving support, understanding and encouragement.*

*This book is also dedicated to the settlers of the Endeavour-Usherville
area, particularly those of the Cheremosz school district. Special
mention is due to those of Ukrainian descent on this 1991/92
centennial year of Ukrainian settlement in Canada*

CONTENTS

acknowledgements—i

introduction—iii

map of Usherville area—vi

ACKNOWLEDGEMENTS

I WOULD LIKE TO EXPRESS MY DEEP APPRECIATION TO Norman Harris for offering his historical knowledge, accuracy and adding texture to this book, and to Patricia Armstrong for encouraging this project from the beginning. My gratitude to Joan Kanigan for sharing her anthropological thesis and to Sinda Shaw and Jeanann Tell for their excellent illustrations.

Special gratitude is also extended to the immediate members of the Rupchan family who so willingly shared their lives: Nick Rupchan, John and Annie Rupchan, George and Helen Rupchan, and Katie (Rupchan) Prestayko.

A sincere thanks to all the relatives, friends, neighbours and acquaintances in the Endeavour-Usherville area and beyond, who helped immeasurably: George Boychuk, Sturgis; Tony Harras, Regina; John Kudeba, Canora; George Wiwcharuk, Usherville; William Wiwcharuk, Preeceville; James Cameron Worcester, Sicamous, B.C.; Wendy Parsons and Zach Dietrich, Moose Jaw; Bill Wihnan, Stenen; Sidor Dembinsky, Endeavour; Elizabeth Seminuik, Regina; Pete Rusnak, Saltcoats; Sam Yurchuk, Calder; Matt Hnatiuk, Bredenbury; Lena Arie, Preeceville; Mary Mostoway, Calder; Emily Maddaford, Saltcoats; Ralph Jarotski, Canora; Lindsay Anderson, Regina; Laddy Martinosky, Gerald; and Robert Bozak, Toronto, Ontario.

I am exceedingly grateful to the Parkland Regional Library system, particularly those in the Yorkton branch without whose diligent perserverance and patient probing I could not have completed this book.

My appreciation also to the Saskatchewan Archives Board for use of photographs, and other important research materials and to the Ukrainian Canadian Museum of Canada in Saskatoon, especially Rose Marie Fedorak and Randal Bodnaryk for their invaluable help with research, photographs, and encouragement.

***

This project has been funded in part by the Ukrainian Canadian Foundation of Taras Shevchenko.

УКРАЇНСЬКА КАНАДСЬКА ФУНДАЦІЯ ІМ. ТАРАСА ШЕВЧЕНКА

I am also profoundly appreciative of the funding provided by the Ukrainian Orthodox Men's Association, Regina, the Ukrainian Canadian Congress, Saskatchewan Provincial Council and to members of the Harris (Haras) family, Norman, Tony and Sharon, Anne, Elsie and Edward for their financial assistance, encouragement and support.

JUDITH SILVERTHORNE

INTRODUCTION

THIS BOOK IS ABOUT HEROES—UNSUNG HEROES FROM our pioneer past. It is a biography which attempts to fill in some of the information gaps which exist in the history of the settlement of western Canada. Among the present generation there is an unforgivable lack of understanding of the hardships that our pioneer forefathers endured. This ignorance has led to a kind of romantic notion of those early years. There is a perception that everybody worked hard, worked in harmony with one another and that everybody prospered.

Policies of various European governments plus poverty brought waves of immigrants. This was the land of opportunity—only the immigrants didn't find it exactly as advertised. This was especially true for eastern Europeans. They settled on some of the poorest land, since many arrived after most of the good land was already occupied. Furthermore they often relied on rumours and old world experiences choosing sandy land, land with sloughs or land with a heavy bush growth. Peter Rupchan with his dream of making pottery found himself on such land struggling to prove his homestead and raise a family.

Diversify, be innovative, find a niche and fill it are clichés that the farming community has heard over the years. No one showed more innovation than Peter Rupchan in his attempt to diversify his income with the sale of pottery. It took an incredible amount of hard work to make pottery.

All his efforts were met with skepticism and ridicule. Being a potter just wasn't the manly thing to do. No one seemed to entertain the idea of a cottage industry in official circles. The pervasive attitude was that Canada needed settlers to fill in the landscapes, the goods they produced to be hauled out via rail. There were several early potters, millers, as well as, Doukhobors with their brick factories. These received no encouragement or recognition. The fact that these cottage industries were started and run by people of eastern European descent almost guaranteed obscurity.

The remaining pieces of pottery that are still to be found in various homes in the Endeavour-Usherville area are monuments to this early pioneer. His dream, although short lived due to his untimely death, lives in each piece. Peter Rupchan along with his brother-in-law Metro (Jim) Safruk live as heroes. They have left us a legacy in the field of crafts that is a unique blend of old world and new. Peter made pots for grinding poppy seeds (makitras), pitchers for raising cream out of milk (hladun) and pots for baking cabbage rolls and verenyky (horschok) plus the various styles of cups, dishes, dolls and whistles. He will be remembered in the local folklore for generations to come.

NORMAN HARRIS
ENDEAVOUR, SASKATCHEWAN
AUGUST, 1991

made in
SASKATCHEWAN

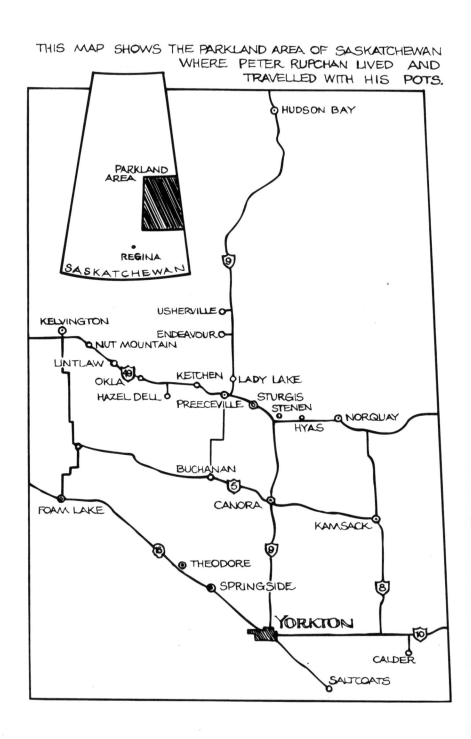

THIS MAP SHOWS THE PARKLAND AREA OF SASKATCHEWAN WHERE PETER RUPCHAN LIVED AND TRAVELLED WITH HIS POTS.

Chapter 1

BEGINNINGS
(1883-1905)

G ENTLY PETER RUPCHAN FINGERED THE SHARD IN HIS rough hands while he surveyed the broken pieces of pottery scattered on the side of the steep ravine below. Had he done the right thing? Maybe he should have sold his entire wagonload of pottery instead of smashing it? After all, in Saskatchewan in the 1930s every penny counted. He wasn't sure any more what was fitting after the unusual events of the past 24 hours.

Late yesterday afternoon he had guided his horses into the Buchanan marketplace. When he brushed away the dirt and leaves to level the ground for his pottery display, his worn hands raked over a bulging wallet. Although the wallet contained $1900, Rupchan, without hesitating, turned it over to the R.C.M.P. The wallet's owner, a prosperous farmer, had held a successful auction sale the day before and after an evening in the bar, had lost his wallet in the stockyards where he had slept in a drunken stupor. The farmer thanked Rupchan for the find, then turned to leave. The police officer called him back, slipped a $50 bill from the wallet and handed it to a delighted Rupchan. Wordlessly the craftsman turned the money over in his trembling hands. The reward money was as much as he could earn in a week selling his wagonload of pottery! All he could think about was going home the fastest way possible. And now, here he was on his way.

Yet Rupchan hesitated. Maybe he had been foolish to destroy his pottery? Perhaps he should have kept all the money in the wallet? He peered down at his worn overalls and his faded shirt. A light layer of dust covered his tattered boots. It was too late now. Quickly he dropped the shard and kicked it into the ravine: Rupchan climbed back into his steel-wheeled wagon and prodded the horses towards Usherville. Lord, he was weary of travelling, tired of struggling. He would be glad to get home to his family. His family! He'd almost forgotten about them. What would he tell everyone about his earlier than expected return? Rupchan churned over the turn of events as the wagon clattered over the stony road near his farm. His wife would be furious!

"You stupid man. You could have sold your pottery to earn even more money, Petro," Safta would admonish as she flapped about like a plump, squawking hen. He would have to admit she was right and once again the fight would be on for him to give up his "pottery foolishness" and go back to farming. He didn't want another argument so perhaps a false tale of good sales was the best solution.

Rupchan sighed. The past day's events summed up his whole life. Unexpected windfalls would come along, followed by adversity. He seemed to rub life the wrong way. Why couldn't he make the right decisions?

At that moment Rupchan decided he would establish himself as a successful potter "come the end of the world or Safta's fury." He was tired of trying to please someone. He had made it this far hadn't he? He guessed he had his early years to thank for strengthening him and helping him to survive in this God-forsaken land. It seemed his whole life had been one long struggle to survive. All he had done was trade one harsh country for another.

The small obscure village of Molodia in Ukraine where Rupchan had been born was as far removed from the vast open prairies of Saskatchewan as one could imagine. It was tucked away within the wide, ever-changing borders of the Austro-Hungarian Empire in the province of Bukovina. Petro's illegitimate arrival on June 17, 1883 into uneducated and impoverished conditions had left him little chance for success or even survival.[1]

His mother Akseniya (Agnes) Vihnan and Nikolai Robchan (Nick Rupchan), whom she later married, struggled hard to raise Peter in an uncompromising society where harsh peasant-like treatment and paltry existence prevailed.² For many under the Austro-Hungarian rule life was filled with endless suffering at the hands of wealthy landowners who had thousands of morge³ of land. The tiny landowners with large families who tried to exist on two and a half or less morge of overworked soil sank farther and farther into hopeless poverty.

The Rupchans had even less security and educational opportunities for Peter were not pursued. To attend school a child had to be registered with the local authorities. And that meant the parents had to pay much higher taxes than those they already could not afford. Although Nikolai found some work as a gardener, he earned little. The Rupchans barely had enough to eat. With the birth of a second son, Wasyl, in 1889 and then another child on the way, they had to do something to improve their conditions. The only possibility for them was to follow the common practice of sending the oldest children off to work as apprentices. So at age seven, Peter was indentured to a local blacksmith.⁴ However, he was unhappy with his situation and soon ran away to join a pottery factory owner who employed eight men. Meanwhile his parents grasped at the opportunity to emigrate and left for Canada in 1899. It is quite probable they had lost touch with Peter, for he remained behind in Ukraine learning the pottery trade.

The factory was located about three miles east of Chernivitsi, some 10 miles from Molodia. Once Peter was older and more experienced he was permitted to travel with the factory owner in the city of Chernivitsi. There he sat in a large yard where the pottery was displayed and sold, watching it to make sure no one stole the earthenware. Peter enjoyed his outing, but the owner was sometimes a harsh instructor. He frequently beat those apprentices who made mistakes. Peter as a young lad had apparently made a number of them.

The beatings only strengthened Rupchan's determination to be independent. He thrived on the creativity of working with clay and vowed one day he would operate his own pottery industry.

Then several years later, at about the age of 20, a shooting incident set his fate. Whether Peter was wounded during a border skirmish while serving in the army or shot in a personal dispute is unclear, but the resulting injury left him unable to bend his left arm to his face. Choices for earning a living became more limited for him, but even with his crippled arm he mastered his trade. He was an accomplished potter when he emigrated to Canada in 1905.

Rupchan, like many immigrants from Europe, found the possiblity of owning his own land in Canada an irresistible opportunity. He shared the dream with three million Europeans who settled the prairies, including the half million who migrated from Ukraine. Many were impoverished and nearly destitute, but the guarantee of almost free land enticed them to pursue the expedition. The severe winters and austere conditions they found on arrival in Canada at times seemed more like a nightmare than an answer to their dreams. Nevertheless, Peter Rupchan saw life in Canada as his only hope for survival. Embarking from Hamburg, Peter stepped confidently and with anticipation onto the shores of the vast new continent 22 days later. From Halifax he headed immediately for the prairies where men were needed to build railways to accommodate the swarming surge of thousands carving out settlements in the west.

(Authors's Note: All footnote references will be found near the end of the book in Appendix 1, Chapter Notes.)

Chapter 2

ADVENTURES
(1905-1908)

H IRED BY THE CN OUT OF CANORA, RUPCHAN HELPED survey and clear township and range cutlines through much of the uninhabited bushland north of Canora. This gave him ample opportunity to assess the land for a suitable homestead site and the raw materials for his pottery operation. But uppermost in Peter's thoughts was to locate his family that had abandoned him as a youngster. He constantly inquired about them as he travelled.

Finally, a full year later, he discovered news that his father was working as a farm labourer at Russell, Manitoba. Rupchan expectantly set out from Yorkton, but after a gruelling three or four day walk found his family had moved several years previously. Determined to find them, Peter trudged the lonesome dirt roads until he finally located them on a gravelly quarter in the Saltcoats-Calder area.[1]

He was gratified to be reunited with his parents, brother Wasyl, and introduced to his 13-year-old sister Veronia. He posed happily with his mother and brother for a photograph in his black breeches, white shirt and vest with a handkerchief loosely tied about his neck. On his head was a fedora; his rifle was propped upright at his side.

Peter's glowing reports of the, as yet, uninhabited lands farther north appealed to his family. They decided to move from the populated Calder area to where there would be room to take out adjoining homesteads. The Endeavour-Usherville area, as it came to be known, was filled with abun-

Peter (on the right) with his mother Akseniya and his brother Wasyl at Calder in 1906.

dant timber for building and firewood. There were bountiful hay meadows and plenty of water for grazing cattle and sheep. Where years before buffalo had roamed the wilderness, vetch hay now grew to the height of a man's chest. The region teemed with waterfowl and wildlife. As there were no plans to cultivate the land the numerous stones wouldn't matter. In fact, they would be useful for building foundations.

And so, at the end of March in 1906, Peter, his brother Wasyl and father Nikolai, all applied for homesteads in the Astwood (now Lady Lake) area, sight unseen. However, after inspecting the land they had chosen without covering of snow they were disappointed to find nothing but dense, scrubby bush, rocks and bogs.[2] By the 18th of May they had all abandoned their homesteads and proceeded farther north to search for more suitable land.

In the meantime a short, stout 18-year-old Ukrainian girl caught the eye of Peter on one of his many working trips through Canora. Married on November 8, 1906, Safta (Sophie) Safruk shyly handed her new husband the customary shevek.[3] She posed for her outdoor wedding picture in a warm sheepskin coat and sturdy boots. A pert box-style hat, called a koshek, with money sewn on the fringes was her only adornment.[4]

Peter, always debonair, wore a fur hat and an open cloth jacket with a scarf thrown carelessly around his neck. His equally sturdy boots and the solemnity in both their expressions was an indication of the grit and determination they would need to face their lives together.

Seven years earlier Safta's family had homesteaded on a site that would later be across the road from the "old" hospital in Canora. Here, Katrina (Katherine) and Diordi (George) Safruk felt was where they would securely remain, but things were to change with the marriage of their one daughter. Their only son, Metro (Jim), would also later play an important role in Rupchan's life. For the time being the Safruks were content to stay where they were, while Peter and Safta trundled off with the rest of the Rupchan family to the latest homestead about a mile north of present day Endeavour.

Safta and Peter Rupchan on their wedding day, November 8, 1906 at Canora.

The Rupchans followed mostly twisting and winding pre-settlement trails previously used by migrating buffalo herds or the horse and cart tracks still in use by the small groups of Indians who travelled through the district. The only other paths were the cleared woodline and range trails that were not as suitable for travelling with oxen and bulky possessions.

The Rupchans—Nikolai and Agnes, Peter and Safta, Wasyl, and Veronia, along with a family of Wiwcharuks, were among the first European settlers to the area to exercise squatters' rights in township 37 between Endeavour and Usherville. At that time the quarter sections had not even been surveyed, in fact the Wiwcharuks built their home on the road allowance line and had to move it when the area became officially opened for settlement in December of 1907.

The areas were gradually opened west by townships from south to north and quickly filled by homesteaders. A steady influx of pioneers continued until after the first world war and a second major wave occurred during the depression years. The first scattered families, however, lived in primitive, isolated conditions.

Wasyl's house where the Rupchan's spent the first winter.

When the Rupchans reached their destination they hastily built a log dwelling on Wasyl's land, on the southwest corner of section 16-37-5-W2 and they all moved in together. Peter applied for the northwest quarter and Nikolai the northeast one, near the South Etoimami River (now the Lilian).

Peter had cleared an acre and a half on his own wooded land but had not yet had time to build a home. Money earned working for the CN and building houses bought four oxen, new harness, a wagon, new machinery and he even had money left over. Things looked rosy for the young Rupchans and Peter had great expectations of soon being able to start on his pottery operation.

One evening in March of 1907 Peter and his stepfather had one of the first of their many disagreements. It was serious enough that Peter, in spite of the biting cold winds and high banks of snow, went out the following day, cleared the snow away and began cutting down trees to build a crude log dwelling.

He hastily built the primitive eight foot by ten foot hovel only a few feet high, then threw some sod, or a thin layer of straw, onto the roof. Scraping the frozen ground, he brought the dirt in to warm it up for making the plaster to fill the cracks. Peter stuck a stovepipe in the center of the roof and within three days he and Safta were living there.

Two weeks later a fire in the middle of the night destroyed their primitive home and $200 worth of provisions. They also lost their naturalization papers. The worst part was that Peter had to apologize to his father and move back in with him for the next two and a half months.

In June Peter began building another home. With Safta expecting their first child he took a little more time and built a larger, sturdier log dwelling, 20 feet wide by 15 feet long. He also seeded his first crop and was the proud owner of one cow, two steers and a calf.

When Nikolai began building a house in the spring of 1908 on his own quarter it became evident he would continue to live in the neighbourhood. Most pioneering families resided close by one another and lived in tight harmony for support and companionship. But not so the Rupchans. Peter and his stepfather constantly disagreed, seemingly about everything.

Nikolai was a strict, serious man of average height, who often sported whiskers. He always spoke in Romanian and stubbornly refused to converse in Ukrainian, the native language of his wife. Communications were stilted at the best of times and Peter was often called upon by his protesting mother to smooth ruffled feathers between the pair.

Akseniya, a tall, capable Ukrainian woman, of 5'8", was usually good-natured and lenient with her children. She never shirked the hard, exhausting work foisted upon her. When she married Nikolai at the age of 18, Peter was almost two-and a half-years-old. The probability that Nikolai was not Peter's father seems, perhaps, to account for his condescending manner and insensitive dealings with his wife and stepson.

Disagreements between father and son continued. By May of 1908 Peter and Safta had abandoned their homestead and newly built house, moving four miles north and a mile east to a gravelly quarter near present day Usherville. Peter took an application out on the homestead in February, rejected it and then reclaimed it again in April. His indecision ended when Peter discovered deposits of silica sand on the new quarter that would benefit his proposed pottery work.

Carefully and energetically Rupchan began to fulfill the requirements to obtain the patent on his new homestead. It became increasingly important for Peter to possess land in his own name as a first step towards establishing a successful pottery business. Besides being proof of his independence, it would give him the freedom to do what he loved best.

Nikolai and Akseniya Rupchan, Peter's mother and stepfather, ca. 1918.

Chapter 3

SURVIVING
(1908-1914)

URVIVING WOULD NOT HAVE BEEN EASY FOR PETER AND Safta in those early colonizing years, even had they remained living near the elder Rupchans. Like all the other early settlers, they found proving a homestead difficult. Using the crude and primitive tools to clear away trees, grub out roots and break the land was only part of the strenuous ordeal.

The Rupchans found it was a constant battle to stop the attacking wildlife that preyed on their domesticated animals and it was necessary to do substantial fencing in the dense bush to keep in straying livestock. In defiance of the elements they attempted to grow crops and hay for their cattle and invariably laboured for enough food to eat. Mostly oats had to be grown due to the poor varieties of wheat and the killing frosts that seldom left enough to thresh. The wheat was often of such poor quality that the chickens did not want to eat it. The Rupchans found every new day that dawned brought more challenging hardships.

One of Rupchan's closest neighbours, Giorgi Skutelnik said, "Plowing with oxen always was a problem. The only fly repellant was a mixture of lard, pine tar, and kerosene or turpentine. This wasn't very effective on hot days as perspiration washed it off. The oxen when pestered by mosquitoes, bull flies and deer flies, headed for the nearest slough. No amount of beating with a switch or pulling on the reins would turn them back to the

fields. It was not an uncommon sight on a hot day to see oxen in full harness and pulling a plow, cooling off in a slough, the owner fuming on the
banks."[1]

Dealing with oxen headed for sloughs was a familiar problem for Peter
as his land had more than its share of water. About 15 to 20 acres were covered by the South Etoimami Lake along with the river that fed it. The
remainder of his land was dense bush, swamps and gravel. He found it a
definite challenge to produce anything.

Loneliness was another problem in the wilds of northeast
Saskatchewan, in particular for Safta. After they moved to Usherville their
only neighbours were the migrating Indians. She was a lonely new mother
after the birth of their first child, a daughter they named Mary. And though
Safta kept busy helping to clear the land with Peter and struggled to grow
an immense garden, she missed socializing. Besides longing for contacts
with other families and communities, she yearned to see her parents and
brother, Metro.

The trips to Canora to visit them were infrequent, as were ventures for
mail or supplies. The Rupchans' nearest post office was at Plateau, 30-35
miles to the south, near present day Sturgis. They had to travel another 30
miles to Canora for their main provisions. Although Peter and his neighbours could easily walk 35-40 miles a day, they only made the trips when
necessary. Major shopping trips with oxen were a slow process and an even
rarer event.

The loneliness for the young Rupchans was partially remedied in 1909
when Safta's parents moved to Usherville. At the time the Safruks felt it
was providence that a Boer War Veteran offered to purchase their quarter
near Canora. Being a recipient of the South African Volunteer Bounty
Land Certificate enabled the man to qualify for two quarters of land anywhere north of Canora that was still open for homesteading. He wanted to
trade. Before Katrina would sign the necessary papers she insisted they
receive an additional $350. Diordi, Katrina and Metro left their comfort-
able lodgings and chose the secluded parcels of land across the road from
Peter and Safta.

Safruks' home built in the Ukrainian style.

The decision to move was one they regretted all their lives, but Safta enjoyed having her mother nearby. A practising midwife, Katrina attended most of her grandchildren's births, and was there to give advice. It was a comfort to mother and daughter to have each other's support and companionship while the men frequently worked away from home.

For Peter the continued grappling to establish a homestead and eke out a living was more than he could bear at times. He struggled hard doing what he disliked, so he could do what he loved. His unceasing desire to be a potter burned within him. As each successive child was born, first Mary in 1908, then Dora in 1909, followed by Nick in 1910 and Agnes (Akseniya, later called Sarah by neighbours and at school) in 1911, Rupchan became concerned with more mouths to feed and more people to support. The chance of being able to work on his pottery seemed remoter all the time.

Peter found it necessary to seek employment in off-farm work in order to raise money to sustain the family. This was the case for everyone in the area. The men generally had only three options available—working on farms, working on the railways or working in the bush. Between 1908 and the first world war the wages were only 50 to 75 cents a day, but at least it was an income.

Peter's sister Veronia with her husband George Seminuik and their son William, ca. 1911.

In October and November of 1908 Wasyl, who was still a bachelor, worked on a section gang near Humboldt, but Peter never joined him there. He was too busy in the very early years proving his homestead to be working far from home. There was a possibility for working at Fulton's sawmill operation only a mile north of Usherville in the Etoimami Valley close to his homestead, but it is doubtful if he was ever an employee.

In the fall it was increasingly common for the settlers to travel south in search of harvest work and Peter was no exception. He went wherever he could find work often walking to the Calder, Saskatchewan area or into Manitoba around the Russell district where friends and relatives hired him.

In August of 1912 the newspapers predicted bumper crops. Advertisements asked for 2500 men to come from the east to help with the harvest. Huron Wheat was excellent and ideal warm weather was ripening grain rapidly. Excess rainfall in the last week of August didn't discourage headlines later that fall from announcing "Saskatchewan Crops Bigger and Better Than Ever." This was in sharp contrast to the headlines reporting the sinking of the luxury liner, Titanic, that caused but a ripple of interest in the hard working communities on the prairies.

It was during this harvest year that Peter, his brother Wasyl and their father were working near Russell as teamsters hauling sheaves. Early on the morning of November 12 the gas-powered tractor quit working. A steamer was brought over from the neighbours to pull the first one. Peter hooked the two tractors together with a short chain. As the machinery started rolling Wasyl unnecessarily jumped down from the rack and landed between the huge wheels of the two tractors as they clanged together.

Peter and his father stood helplessly watching in horror as Wasyl's squashed body staggered several steps then keeled over. Nikolai was devastated, and although offered some monetary compensation for the loss of his son, decided to sue the owners for a larger amount. He was unsuccessful in this attempt and came away without any compensation. Instead he brought Wasyl's crushed body home and laid him to rest in the St. Demitrius Greek Orthodox Church cemetery on the hill east of Lady Lake. He was 24.

Ironically just two months before his death, Wasyl had received the patent for his homestead, as had Nikolai.[2] Meanwhile Peter was still anxiously fulfilling the prerequisites for his homestead. He managed to break five acres in 1908 and seven the following year, cropping all 12 acres in 1909 and 1910 without breaking any more during those years. He improved seven acres during each year of 1911 and 1912, and by the end of 1913 Rupchan was industriously farming a total of 26 acres. He had also done extensive fencing.

The Rupchans chose the top of a hill to build their third house, a large log structure about 24 by 34 feet long, a portion of which became a workshop for Peter's pottery business. One end was the kitchen and the middle section was for bedrooms and storage. To the east of the house a 10 foot by 12 foot shed held grain and various tools, and a peetch (clay oven) was built behind it. About 100 yards to the west of the house at the bottom of the knoll Peter constructed a 44 foot square stable for their five cows and two oxen. Beside it ran a creek where he dug a shallow well and inserted a wooden barrel for a cribbing.

Nick, his oldest son, was curious about the well as any six- or seven-year-old lad might be and immediately investigated. While peering down the hole, he leaned too far and fell into the water with a resounding splash. In a panic, flailing his arms and kicking his legs in the tiny confines of the cribbing, he gulped for air and yelled for help. His older sisters who were nearby heard his shouts. Luckily he still wore their hand-me-down dresses. They grabbed him by the hem and hauled him out. It was one of the few times he was glad there was no money to buy him a pair of trousers.

Money was scarce throughout the community and although Nick finally received a pair of pants when he started school several years later at the age of 10, he attended classes for only 18 months. There were not enough funds for taxes to keep the school open.

Rupchan initially concentrated on making his farm a viable operation, but the desire to make pottery became an obsession. He began to spend every spare moment walking and scouring the countryside for suitable clay. The fine sand he needed to mix with the clay was available and plentiful on

Rupchan's children, Agnes and Nick, dressed for a special occasion, ca. 1919.

his own quarter. The clay itself was more difficult to find. Using only a spade he dug sample holes all over his farm and throughout the southern part of the Etoimami valley.

One cool autumn day Peter was anxiously searching for clay north of the Safruks' farm. The ground was slightly hard from early frosts and Peter found digging difficult. He had spent the morning scooping out several holes. Down every few inches he'd take a sample of the dirt and roll it in his hands contemplatively, only to throw it away in disgust, then dig deeper, or move on to the next spot.

Rupchan decided he would try one more hole. There, that was deep enough, he thought. He crouched down to grab a sample of the earth pressing it this way and that between his calloused fingers. Excitedly he seized another handful patting it from palm to palm, then squeezing it into different shapes. He sat back on the heels of his weathered boots. Yes, this was it!

It had taken Peter two years, but at last he was triumphant. He began fashioning all the necessary pottery equipment from scratch using his ingenuity and experience gained in the old country. Peter was delighted when Safta's brother, Metro, showed interest in the pottery operation. His father-in-law also seemed agreeable. With a chisel, Diordi chipped Peter's first grinding stone. It was perfect for pulverizing the clay to a suitable consistency for throwing pots.

It seems likely that at first Peter used Safta's peetch for baking small test batches of his earthenware. Needing more space, he eventually constructed a four by eight foot stone kiln for firing. His neighbour at the time, John Kudeba, said one of Rupchan's early firing methods was to heat his pottery for two days, cover it with dirt, and leave it for a week until it cooled.[3]

Peter began selling his pots locally. He eventually planned to expand and travel with his wares but for the time being he thought it best if he concentrated on farming and establishing his homestead. At the same time he could experiment with pottery and settle into a routine with Safta and the children.

It was in the fall of 1913 when the Safruks received the certificate of title to their half section. The following year on March 30, 1914 an ecstatic Peter at last acquired the patent to his land. The two families felt fairly secure. They had survived the first gruelling years.

Chapter 4

TRAGEDIES
(1914-1916)

THRILLED WITH SECURING HIS HOMESTEAD AT LAST,
Peter felt free to pursue his creative nature and establish himself as
a productive potter. Still there were many obstacles to overcome
and the difficulties of everyday living had to be faced by Peter and those
around him.

When the first world war broke out the young Rupchans and the
Safruks were securely settled into their simple yet demanding routine lives.
They were surrounded by more settlers and the first Usherville post office
opened several miles to the south.[1] The town of Preeceville sprang up and
although some supplies were available there, it was still preferable to travel
to Canora for a wider selection of goods.

Safta's father made one such languorous journey with oxen to Canora
for groceries during the early spring of 1914. Unfortunately the return trip
was through pouring rain. Soaked, the 56-year-old Diordi caught a severe
cold. He lay for three months at home racked with pneumonia before he
died.

Although his death was devastating blow for Katrina, she rallied and
prudently divided the half section of land between their offspring, Safta and
Metro. She continued to live in her home with her son Metro, who was still
a bachelor.

Peter's life too was drastically affected. Without Diordi to advise him
Rupchan generously agreed to co-sign a loan for a neighbour wanting to

buy some horses. A mortgage was registered on Peter's highly-prized homestead by the Bank of Toronto in Preeceville that July. Trusting in the fellow's integrity to pay his debts Peter was unconcerned and continued to operate his pottery business.

Debt, obtaining homesteads, earning a viable income and all the hardships that went along with it were not the only concerns of the early settlers. William Wiwcharuk, a resident in the area said, "Somewhere between 1910 and 1915 a crime wave swept the area. Many oxen were stolen. My father lost an ox at that time. Others lost two or three which meant a great loss to the homesteader. The thieves, in typical western fashion, would butcher the oxen and haul it to Canora, or anywhere where they could sell it. The police finally caught the thieves and the thefts stopped."[2]

Two men known to be involved in the cattle rustling ring stayed at Nikolai Rupchan's home for a time. Totally innocent, Peter was not aware his stepfather had any knowledge of the crimes until one wintry morning. Mounted police from Preeceville began investigating the disappearance of three or four big oxen from the Safruks' the night before. The oxen tracks in the freshly-fallen snow led from Safruks' barn, a mile west past Peter's yard to the slaughter site next to the river that wound past Nikolai's land. The departing sleigh tracks led straight to his home. Although Nikolai denied any involvement it was one more reason for Peter to disassociate himself from his unscrupulous stepfather.

Crimes like these were one of the repercussions of the destitution everyone faced in early settlement. While the first world war raged and rationing of food became the order of the day, it meant little to most in the Endeavour-Usherville area. They simply had no money to buy anything anyway. Lack of cash even to pay taxes or the $10 homestead fee caused many to lose their land and homes.

It was not surprising then that Peter felt the economic strain of the times and became even more determined to keep his alternate means of earning a living. He never deluded himself that his pottery business would be the sole moneymaker, nor did he feel his talents were to be recognized in any artistic sense. Even minute amounts of cash were hard for his customers to scrape together, and purchasing art was the farthest thing from their

minds. Peter loved the creative aspects of making pottery and with his for-
mal training produced the practical pieces that his customers wanted and
could afford in those difficult times. Good, solid cooking vessels were what
they needed and bought. With pots selling from five cents to 35 cents apiece
Peter was able to supplement his income so he did not have to resort totally
to farming for which he was not the least bit suited.

It didn't take a genius, Peter had decided, to figure out he lacked the moti-
vation to manage a viable agricultural operation. He just had no interest in it.
He knew a little about raising animals and although he worked hard physically
he simply preferred making pottery to earning a living with farming.

Actually, farming in the early 1900s could hardly be called earning a living though it did give an existence of sorts. There was little else to bring in
an income of any kind for the rural world of northeastern Saskatchewan.

Norman Harris, a respected local historian from the Endeavour-
Usherville area, explained the situation. "The people out here, a lot of them
made homebrew for a living because there was no form of employment.
Grain farming only became practical after 1933 in Endeavour. The railway
track went through in '28 and the elevators were built about 1932-33.
Nineteen-thirty-three was the year they could really sell grain and even then
most people didn't have more than 15-20-35 acres."

Selling cordwood was also impractical until after the railway went
through. It just took too long with the oxen to travel the 22 miles to the line
at Preeceville.

"I have an economic survey of this area done in 1941," Harris went on.
"The average size of a farm was 50 acres, so how could a person live on that?
People worked in the bush which at best was $30 a month. It was definately
cheaper or more profitable to make homebrew. With all the big sawmills
they had a ready market.

"Even during the '30s some of the train crew members, the conductor
and passengers were taking homebrew from this area," continued Harris.
"All you had to do was take a couple of gallons to Usherville and the crew
picked it up as if it was crated eggs. I'm not sure what the arrangement was
but they were transporting it for someone else to the cities or to Yorkton
because this is where Bronfmans had a distillery operation."[3]

Rupchan's neighbours almost all made illicit whisky for one reason or another, but he never did. Instead he concentrated on doing some farming and cutting cordwood, neither of which satified his creative inner desires. He prefererred utilizing his training from Ukraine as a potter for diversifying his income. He liked being his own boss and because of his artistic bent, he never gave up the idea of being a truly successful potter. When Safta gave birth to another son in 1915, they named him Bill after Peter's deceased brother Wasyl (William). By then Peter was well on his way to establishing himself as a local craftsman and vendor of pottery. He had recently set up his studio, built new shelving and had designed an excellent throwing wheel.[4]

Then disaster struck when the borrowing neighbour failed to make his loan payments and the bank forclosed. On May 12, 1916 Rupchan lost his land.

Chapter 5

RESTORATION
(1916-1919)

Peter was shocked! His life-long dreams all seemed to be ending in disaster. Totally unprepared for this twist of fate, Rupchan was utterly stunned and disheartened. His very survival was in jeopardy.

Then, while the Rupchans were still reeling from the loss of their land, some salvation arrived. They received permission from James Fraser, a resident of Preeceville who bought their quarter from the bank for $800, to move their buildings.[1] The logical place was across the road to the quarter that Safta had been given by her mother (the SW quarter of section 3, township 38, in range 5.) It was far from satisfactory for Peter to live on land in his wife's name, but he had no other choice. Accordingly, plans were set in motion.

Several loyal neighbours like Pete Kuzuhar, Mike Hnatiuk, Gregory Seminuik, John Federuik, Harry Lysan, and George Skutelnik helped with the relocation. Safta, once again pregnant, made the meals for the working crew.

"It took most of the summer to move," recalled Peter's oldest son, Nick, who was about eight at the time. As each structure in turn was being moved the family slept in one of the still-standing buildings until everything was transferred and rebuilt.

Log by log the house, summer kitchen, barn, granaries and shop were dismantled. First the roof was taken off in sections, placed on skids and pulled with oxen to the other farm. Then the timbers were numbered, moved and reassembled one at a time. When Rupchan decided to divide the combination house and workshop into two buildings they used cross-cut saws to split the large roof.

Peter eventually added a porch area to the diminished house and built a three foot square, 12 foot high chimney—like a fireplace—inside it. He placed his pottery workshop about 100 yards straight east of the house. The barn, pig pen, chicken coops, and a woodpile were scattered in between the two main buildings. Sometime later a low log structure, a buda, with its door facing north, was built to provide sleeping accommodations for some of the older boys.

Although Peter spent the next two years industriously re-establishing the farm, he was totally discouraged. Clearly farming was not for him. It seemed all the more important to him now to concentrate his efforts on setting up an exclusive pottery business as his main method for survival.

"When he moved to SW3 he wouldn't farm anymore," said Nick. "He seemed heartbroken."

Rupchan re-established on the SW3-38-5-W2. [Saskatchewan Archives Board Photo #R-A1045(2)]

The remains of Rupchan's workshop on the SW3. The kiln was inside to the right. [Saskatchewan Archives Board #R-A 1045(6)]

Everyone in the family agrees Rupchan never again genuinely farmed as a livelihood. For the longest time Peter just continued to function from day to day, lethargically doing the necessary work, while the family, newly installed in their current abode, once again fell into a domestic routine. In October Safta gave birth to another son, Metro (Jim), named after her brother.

Then tragedy struck again. A deadly influenza epidemic spread through the district leaving no family untouched. Even if the medical help had been available to serve the isolated settlements, they could have done nothing to stop the multitudes of people dying from the flu and pneumonia epidemics that broke out periodically through the next several decades. Although complications would be treatable after 1940 when the antibiotic penicillin was discovered, a cure for the dreaded influenza had not then, nor indeed has ever been found. The worst attack was to be the "Spanish Influenza" which struck a major death toll of over 20,000,000 people worldwide from 1918 to 1919. But even by 1916 numerous families in the Endeavour-Usherville district had already been devastated by various influenza viruses, including Peter and Safta's.

The only medicines around to ease the suffering were generally home-made ones like homebrew boiled with honey, garlic poultices, Hoffman drops and nervaline. The overworked doctor, when and if he was available, was fetched by Metro Kudeba, who had the only car in the area. Kudeba also brought any medicines available to the sick people, until he, too, died in 1918.

The entire Rupchan household came down with the flu except Peter, who throughout his life was seldom sick. Safta lay deathly ill for two weeks. Their son Nick was sick for only a day or so and it fell to him to rock the infant, Jim, in the cradle. Peter was kept busy checking on the neighbours' stock. He walked seven or eight miles each day to water and feed the cattle in the area, then went home and cared for his own family.

One wintry day while making his rounds he came across a neighbour wrapped in her sheepskin coat, frozen in the snow. On investigating their home he found her husband had also died. Peter fed and cared for their three young boys until their grandmother from Canora arrived to rescue them several days later.

Soon afterwards three members of Peter's own family also perished: one-year-old Bill, Mary, aged seven, and her six-year-old sister, Dora. Only half of their children, Nick, Agnes, and Jim, survived. The Rupchans spent a totally despondent winter adjusting to their tragedies and slowly recovering from their illnesses. From losing their land to the decimation of their family, 1916 had indeed been a disastrous year!

The next few years were far from idyllic either. In October of 1918 John was born after a very wet summer when little hay could be made due to the weather. The winter proved very long and cold and by the spring of 1919 all the animals were starving. People resorted to taking thatch off the roofs of their buildings to feed the livestock. By spring feeble looking animals stood beside granaries with the rafters bare.

The humans were not much better off and often wondered why they were there and what they were doing? Grain prices were low with wheat only paying six cents a bushel and oats four cents, while the cost of a new plow in 1916 was $26. It was hard to juggle income and expenses, a most depressing condition for everyone concerned. In particular it affected Peter who resumed the only distraction that pleased him—his pottery.

Chapter 6

POTTERY OPERATIONS
(1919)

IS SPIRITS TOTALLY BROKEN, RUPCHAN IMMERSED himself in his pottery, only this time on a much grander scale. After a phenomenal amount of painstaking work, he made his operation viable. Of primary importance to Peter was the construction of a substantial one room kiln next to his workshop.

First he levelled the ground. Then using the numerous rocks found locally, he placed flat gray stones on the bottom, making sure not to use limestone. Rupchan added a layer of coarse gravel, then filled in the cracks and smoothed wet clay over the entire floor. The curved stone wall structure he assembled on top was plastered with similar mud inside and out. Heat from firing the pots gave the inside shell of clay a hard brick-like consistency.

With the help of another neighbour, Roman Korney, Rupchan bent a section of iron to frame the doorway of the eight foot wide kiln. He fashioned a chimney hole three quarters of the way up one end of the kiln to allow smoke and excess moisture to escape. Within a couple of years the kiln began to show signs of deterioration, so Rupchan assembled a partial roof of boards and rails around it to keep it protected from the elements.

The care taken in building his kiln was typical of the methodical approach Peter employed in his operation from start to finish. First he hauled home a wagonload of the dark clay, then either went himself or sent his son, Nick, to the quarter across the road to bring back some pails of silica sand.

Rupchan's kiln on the SW3-38-5-W2. [Saskatchewan Archives Board Photo #R-A 1045(3)]

The moist earthy smell filled Rupchan's nostrils for the next two or three days as he stirred the damp clay and stamped it with his feet to break up the lumps.

Next, using a measurement of approximately two dippers of clay to one of sand, he blended the two ingredients together. The sand not only kept the clay from becoming too sticky to handle, but was also used as a temper.[1] It usually fell to the older children to grind and sift the mixture of clay. This procedure

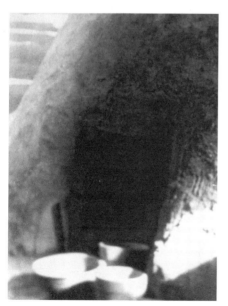

ensured the removal of any stones that would otherwise cause the pots to crack when they were baked. Then Rupchan transferred the clay mixture to a plank platform underneath the window in his workshop and water was added. Peter mixed it with his feet until it was the right consistency. Once prepared, the clay was kept moist under wet gunny sacks and there the aging process began.

Doorway of kiln. Note the size of the opening in relation to the pottery.

Peter Rupchan at work in his pottery studio. [Saskatchewan Archives Board Photo #R-A 1045(5)]

Rupchan formed a portion of the smooth, wet mass of clay into a huge flat slab about three feet by six feet. Using part of a broken scythe he shaved it into one-eighth inch slices to feel if there were any stones remaining. This also made the clay more homogeneous and the wedging, once the clay was divided into intended pot-sized allotments, helped remove air bubbles from the clay. The measured mounds of clay were then stacked within easy reach beside his potter's wheel.

Peter said, "...When I knead the clay for two whole days and then cut it with a scythe blade and again knead it, my arm bothers me a lot, but the rest of the work is not so hard." When asked if he had to knead it that long he replied, "Oh, yes. First I sift the clay and throw out pieces of limestone and other objectional matter. Then I grind the clay and mix different varieties. Adding water, I knead it for two whole days. My wife helped me for some time but it was too hard for her. Now I do it all myself. I cut it in strips and examine it, then knead it again. I keep cutting strips off till there are no streaks in the clay and it is as soft as live rubber, then it's ready for the potter's wheel."[2]

The remains of Rupchan's wheel.

Before he began a day in his workshop, Peter, dressed in overalls and a shirt with the sleeves rolled up to his elbows, donned a huge butcher-style apron that tied at his back. Each morning he started by kneading and forming the lumps of clay required for the day so he could continue spinning pot after pot without having to stop to prepare each piece. He found a constant temperature of 65 degrees F ideal for working with the pliable, smooth clay.

Rupchan assembled his potter's wheel by attaching a three foot diameter lower wooden disk and a somewhat smaller upper turntable onto a rotating metal shaft. He worked the kick-wheel mostly with his bare feet, although sometimes he'd wear a soft moccasin-type shoe.

Rupchan loved the feel of the smooth damp clay between his worn and capable hands. His left arm, although stiff from the gunshot injury incurred in Ukraine as a young man, did not prevent him from expertly shaping flawless pots. As fast as his nimble hands and feet could work he shaped pot after pot perfectly. Masterfully he transformed the crude clay into useable vessels, cups, saucers, plates, bowls, flower pots, candlesticks, vases, urns, and teapots.

"Horschoks," used for souring cream and "miktras" for grinding poppy seeds were some of his best sellers. Outdoor ovens were widely used and many people required different sized baking pots ranging from quarts to three or four gallons to feed their large families. He'd try anything a customer wanted, even a dish for feeding a dog.

As he expertly finished each vessel he removed it from the wheel with a violin string, using a finer, thin brass wire for the fancier ones. Each piece he carefully placed on a shelf where it was allowed to dry thoroughly, then he set the crockery in the kiln for baking.

Sometimes he decorated the pieces before they were "leather hard."[3] Peter placed the pots back on the wheel and by rolling a gear, cogwheel or sprocket around the inside or outside of the pot he imprinted a pattern on the surface of the clay. He used whatever gadgets he could find to decorate his pieces, even sticks and other sharp objects. Purposely he created ridges on the inside of the makitras to facilitate the grinding of poppy seeds.

Most of his pots were carefully fashioned on his pottery wheel, but occasionally he used molds made from rotten tree stumps. First Peter cut the stump at its base, hollowed out the inside and made it smooth. Finally he cut the piece vertically into two or three parts and attached fastenings to rejoin them. "He'd make the bottom out of clay first and then fill the rest around with clay about this thick," said his son John, holding his fingers about an inch apart. He smoothed the additional clay against the sides of the mold to form the vessel walls. "Once it dried, he'd take the clamps away and he'd have a big crock."

One of the largest items Peter tried to make was a cream can. It is doubtful if he made any money on it because of the huge amount of clay it took. In the end when the owner filled it with cream and lifted it off the ground, the bottom gave way.

Peter successfully made toys and dolls for children using tin molds he found in local nuisance grounds. He filled the front and back halves with clay leaving them to dry enough to maintain their shape. Then he removed the mold and joined them by re-dampening the edges and smoothing the clay together.

Mold made from a tree stump.

The finished crock in Norman Harris' hand.

A favourite of the children were the pig, rooster or chicken whistles Rupchan created. The rounded rooster body, made using a broken tin form, had a small squarish hole at the top for a mouthpiece and a larger more rectangular one on the side. The pig had a place to blow along the side. Sometimes he gave the whistles away as free gifts to entice customers to buy his wares, at other times just because he was a generous man.

Rupchan mostly enjoyed throwing pots on his wheel. He was so quick at it he would challenge the neighbourhood men to roll a cigarette while he threw the bottom dish of a flowerpot. Peter always won.

Besides the labour-intensive preparation in handling the clay from raw product to finished pots, Rupchan spent many long hours cutting enough firewood to fire the kiln. He brought home dry or dead logs, whatever he found in the forest. Occasionally he had to use wood which was still slightly damp. His pottery as a result sometimes wasn't fired hot enough or even enough.[4] Rupchan soon learned all of his time would be wasted if the baking wasn't done properly and the pots were underfired. He had to relearn how to fire the kiln for each type of clay he used.

KILN ON
THE SW3 · 38 · 5 · W2

The kiln held approximately 500 articles. Rupchan piled one on top of two others, with the larger pieces placed below and smaller items on top in brick-like fashion. The spaces between allowed the heat to penetrate in and around each piece. The kiln was about eight feet wide on the bottom, where the four rows of pots were stacked in long rows three feet high. Eight to ten inches was left on either side of the stacks, for Rupchan to light fires down the whole length. He used a long pole to push in the three foot long, split firewood.

"The kiln was warmed during the first day to remove any excess moisture in the pottery. Then the pottery was fired until the pieces "glowed red-hot...."[5]

"It took two nights and three days for baking. I don't know when he was sleeping," said his son John, who sometimes helped his father with his work. "He started a little fire first, very slowly or the pots would crack. He increased it day and night and then about the second day or so he would start decreasing the fire and open the draft a little bit—not too far or it would crack for sure."

Rupchan had several simple methods for gauging the proper temperature while he fired steadily for an estimated 72 hours. "He made sure there was a blue flame, which was perfect for firing," said Nick. "He kept adding wood to keep the blue flame." By peering through a small chimney opening in the kiln, he could see the condition of his pots. Once the blue flame was reached, he would close the steel door tightly, lean a stick against it and let it continue baking until the fire died down.

Several hours after the firing, Rupchan slowly opened the door and crawled in to look at the pottery. A flick of his finger against the pot would tell if it was baked enough. If he heard a hollow sound rather than a thump he declared it done. After about 24-48 hours of cooling he directed his older sons to go into the kiln and start unloading. If unloaded too soon, the pots cracked in the cooler outside air.

"All the pottery was red, just like iron gets hot in a stove. It was still hot when we went to take it out," said John, who often had the job of pulling the pottery from the kiln. "It was so hot in there the sweat was pouring from you." Nick also recalls taking the pots from the kiln with a rag because they were so hot.

While the pots were still warm, Rupchan decorated them with glaze. When he was finished, he fired the earthenware for another 12 hours. At last they were finished. The whole operation from raw earth to baked pots took Peter about two weeks to complete. Then he packed the crockery into a hay or straw-lined wagon box ready for sale.

A collection of Rupchan pottery.

Chapter 7

INVENTIONS
(1923-1930)

RUPCHAN LOVED WORKING ON HIS POTTERY, BUT WAS still depressed about losing his homestead. Collaborating with his brother-in-law, Metro, helped alleviate the misery.

Metro, who remained a bachelor all his life, was a pleasant, amusing man and an industrious worker. He farmed on the adjacent land to the young Rupchans and often joined them in work and fun. He particularly enjoyed playing tunes on the accordion. In his early years he had learned the rudiments of the English language from a priest in Canora. Later he bought a

Metro Safruk (l) and Peter Rupchan (r) at the base of the single windmill, ca. 1923.

Ukrainian-English dictionary and painstakingly learned how to read and write English well. People often asked for his help to decipher instruction manuals for setting up machinery and the like. He was willing to assist wherever he could and was always open to new ideas including a few of his own.

When he joined forces to make Rupchan's pottery business a success the pair devised various contraptions in the hopes of making their everyday lives easier. The plan was to employ the natural resources around them.

In 1923 Metro decided to harness the wind and began work on a windmill he placed strategically on a hill by his home. Starting with eight-inch square planks hewn with a broad axe, he built a base on skids. Next he constructed the tower and added huge homemade rotating blades. He activated the windmill by turning it into the direction of the wind using a pry pole.

Metro and Peter cheerfully experimented with the windmill first as a source of power to operate a small grinding mill for flour. This idea seems to have had some measure of success, but using it to run a wood saw proved to be a disappointment.

"They could have sawed it faster with a Swede saw," said Nick, who was a young teenager when his father and uncle began their eccentric experi-

mentations. Undaunted by this slight failure, the pair had more grandiose schemes planned to save themselves time and work. In the end they spent more time and worked harder pursuing their ideas.

To the west of Peter's house, on a little knoll, they built a second windmill about 1927. This time they designed and constructed a 10 foot square log building that sat on a platform about four feet off the ground, leaving space for the huge shaft and gear, like the rear end of a

Single windmill on Metro Safruk's farm.

Double windmill on Rupchan's farm, already damaged by the wind, ca. 1927.
[Saskatchewan Archives Board Photo #R-A 1045(4)]

car, that would operate it. Then they attached two oversized propellers with massive handmade blades on the roof and fashioned a huge belt about 25 feet long that went around both propeller shafts and attached to a wooden pulley. The belt was made from old used tires.

"They didn't peel the tires, just left the grips on and everything," said Nick, who recalls the tires were just turned backwards and laced together. "The belt had to bend and take so much more strain."

The huge propellers ran the large grinding stones inside the building. Here there was a built-in spout for the pulverized clay to fall into a container. Although Peter used this windmill mostly for grinding his pottery clay, when he cleaned the stones he ground wheat into household flour for Safta and the occasional neighbour.

"I sawed wood on the corner here on the outside," said John indicating yet another use of the resourceful structure.

Peter and Metro together could turn the huge windmill into the direction of the wind. Unless the wind was too strong. Then horses turned the gangly structure at the corners. One of the main problems was that the wind would change, commented John, "I remember it didn't work very easy."

"And if there was no breeze they wouldn't do anything at all," added Nick, chuckling. "The windmills were mostly toys the older men played with." Toys or not, the pair put immense energy into making the windmills work, but eventually had to leave the double-bladed one in a stationary position.

"After a while we just had to wait for a south wind. We didn't turn it, it was too heavy for the horses and it broke everything," explained John. "It was kind of propped up in each corner and if you took them away, it was loose and it would hit the ground."

Each night after use, the blades needed to be locked up in case of strong wind gusts. "We had to go and put bricks between the wings and support them with a heavy pole. Somehow or other we tied it up, but it would start to wobble in the wind. I must have broke one of the wings and they had more wobble," explained John. One breezy night someone forgot entirely to lock up the wings. The next morning the smashed blades were found over a quarter of a mile away having landed like pick-up sticks strewn across the fields. So ended this episode of Rupchan's windmill experiments, but perhaps, it was not his last wind-powered structure.

Numerous local people were aware of Rupchan's escapades, but one person to note Rupchan's windmills came about through a different manner entirely. While Peter was investigating various means of glazing and decorating his pottery, he wrote to Professor W. G. Worcester, head of the ceramic engineering department at the University of Saskatchewan in Saskatoon.[1]

Although the professor is no longer living, his son, James Cameron Worcester, also very much a part of the pottery world in Saskatoon, recalls receiving Rupchan's letter and consequently visiting him with his father in 1930. He was greatly intrigued by one of Rupchan's windmills and wrote:

"...The windmill was of Dutch design. Though huge for a prairie windmill, it was not as large as its Dutch counterpart. Mr. Rupchan said he used a horse or team to revolve the mill into the wind, whenever there was a shift in the wind and he needed the mill in operation "

According to Worcester, the particular windmill they saw in 1930 was not the double-bladed one on top of a building, which by that time had no doubt been destroyed, nor was it the single one constructed on a hill by Metro's home. The windmill they recall was in Rupchan's farm yard close to the house and barn. It was a single one with four big Dutch blades and was mounted on a turntable to be turned by horses into the wind.

Rupchan was tenacious and possibly this was another windmill he erected after the destruction of his huge double one. He was forever experimenting to create successful power apparatuses, but eventually he had to accept defeat with wind-powered operations. However, he did not give up inventing contraptions to facilitate the more mundane aspects of his work.

Although, after the demise of his windmills, he was forced to return to using good old-fashioned foot power to mix his clays; later he was able to buy a gas motor which he adapted to aid in grinding clay. He never used the motor for making glazes, his family declared. Besides the problems of modifying the motor for the task, he simply didn't need to use it, as he persistently experimented and made an endless variety of grinding stones throughout his life. There was always one available to facilitate in his methods of making glazes. One such revision of his ideas developed into what was perhaps his most ingenious, yet simple, invention.

In the early years Rupchan sparingly applied a primitive brown glaze that was perhaps more for utilitarian use of sealing the porous pots than for adornment. Then he gradually progressed to more creative glazing using yellow designs and stripes. As his interest in decorating his pottery increased, so did his travels for finding substances to use for surface colours and at one point he even travelled as far away as PeePaw Lake.[2]

He experimented using the primary techniques he had learned in the old country. As time went by his desire was to be more creative and use glazes more elaborately, besides finding an easier method of making them. This was when he contacted Professor Worcester, who decided to personally inspect Rupchan's techniques.

Professor Worcester and his son discovered Rupchan's operation was quite rudimentary compared to the more sophisticated ceramic industry to which they were accustomed. James Worcester recalls:

"...it was a sweltering hot day in August, 1930. We arrived at the farm in the early evening. When we opened the car doors we were met by more mosquitoes than I had ever seen in all my life; the air was black with them and you could hear a constant dull hum. The few farm horses and cows in the yard all huddled around several mosquito smudges trying to keep in the smoke in the hopes of fending off a few of the biting pests.

We met Mr. Rupchan and he took us on a tour of his pottery and gave us an explanation of his operation. He secured his clay from somewhere on his farm. It was a sandy, common, red brick material, not in any sense pottery clay. When fired it was a pale salmon colour, the texture being quite gritty, like sandpaper. He told us he turned his pottery on a homemade kick wheel, an art no doubt learned in his homeland. After digging his clay, he mixed it with water in a shallow wooden box about six feet long, four wide and eight inches deep. He fired his pottery in a primitive wood-burning kiln, located outdoors, I seem to recall. He said he made his pottery when he was not too busy on the farm.

"In the summer he loaded a wagon with his pottery, driving about the country in hopes of selling it. As I recall, most of his pottery consisted of simple bowls, pitchers and like items for use in a kitchen. I can well imagine many of his neighbours and customers had come from Russia and Europe and were accustomed to using this type of kitchen earthenware. This pottery of course was unglazed and as a result would not be water proof. At that time he could not have given his pottery to anyone that had not been accustomed to similar earthenware. Today, no doubt, people who collect antiques would find his pottery valuable and desirable. While we were at the farm we saw no evidence of any of his pottery that might be classed as 'art pottery' for art's sake alone, it was all useful in some way.

"Dad discussed glazes and glazing with him, but with his primitive way of firing his pottery and the quality of clay he had to use, it is doubtful he even was able to successfully decorate his pottery with glazes. I do not believe Dad ever heard from him again after our visit to the farm. I should point out that we saw no evidence of his incising any form of decoration on his pottery, a form of decoration used by early primitive Indians."[3]

Although the Worcesters saw no indication that Rupchan decorated or finished his pottery in any way, neighbours recall buying his pots with glazes and designs on them as early as 1922. It is a certainty Peter did not purchase any commercial glazes as they would have been too costly for his cottage industry. Instead he used his ingenuity. With the desire to incorporate a technique for glazing on a much grander scale, it was only logical that Rupchan set out to overcome the problem. In the end he created one of his most useful inventions.

It was a derrick-like device that he built for crushing glass to produce the glazes. Located just outside his workshop, it was operated through the boards on the roof covering the kiln, recalled Nick, whose job it was to stand inside the shelter and pull the rope.

Rupchan scoured the nuisance grounds and ditches collecting old bottles, jars, broken window panes and any usable glass. Sometimes he hired children to look for the discarded glass or quartz stones, paying them with the toys and whistles he made from clay.

Once collected he put the same coloured glass through a door into a 15 inch square box which sat underneath a crane and heavy weights. A big flat stone rested on the bottom of the box and a 200-pound square piece of iron sized to fit in the box travelled down an eight-foot chamber to smash the glass. He attached the weight to a post with a bolt that had to be replaced often because it broke with the impact of the smashing. When he pulled a rope, then released it, the weight dropped on a dozen or so bottles at a time. Opening the door, he pushed away the coarser pieces, crushing them again. The finer portions he removed with a brush and put into an 18-inch diameter grindstone, which he had chiselled out. It had a shaft in the center and a piece of two inch by four inch studding to lift it.

There Rupchan pulverized the glass fragments into fine powder like flour. Then adding water to the powder to make a paste, he diluted it three or four times until it was like cream. The glaze was then ready to be used.

Rupchan also collected old copper articles, melting them at the same time the pottery was baked. Later he ground the copper finely and mixed it with the powdered glass which resulted in various shades of green glaze depending on the differing amounts of the copper added. He even pulverized lead plates from old batteries for use in colouring the paints and low-ering the melting point.

With the knowledge he'd gleaned from using lead-based glazes in Eastern Europe he was able to utilize the various substances available to him in Saskatchewan. He created colours ranging from shades of brown, tan, yellow, and green to blues and purple. The various minerals and oxides found in the local clay he used as an adhesive for mixing in his glazes affected the colour produced, as did the ground glass, lead and copper.

While his crockery was still warm Rupchan glazed it. Sometimes he dipped the whole pot into the glaze, but more often he painted on designs. He expanded his decorative touches somewhat when he discovered that the use of an ox horn with the tip drilled out and a feather stuck inside was just the tool he needed to apply decorative strips of glaze around his pots. He found he could vary the thickness of the lines by using different sized open-ings in the tips of the horns. Filling the horn with paint, he drew on lines, flower motifs or three and four leaf clovers. He had a steady hand and could deftly brush on the glazes in abstract patterns while the pot was slowly rotat-ing on the wheel.

This decorative glazing no doubt helped with the sale of his pots. In later years he almost always glazed his crockery except for the flower pots, although some of his last batches he left unglazed, for whatever reason.

His inventions at times succeeded in more ways than one. Not only did they serve useful purposes for his work, but they certainly took his mind off the loss of his farm. At least for a time.

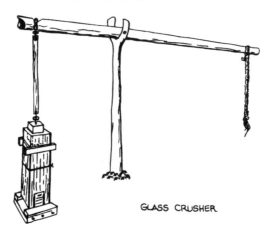

GLASS CRUSHER

Chapter 8

TRAVELLING PEDDLER
(1920-1930s)

"Pots for sale," Rupchan called loudly, as he heaved a huge crock on his head and began walking slowly up the street. "There's pots for sale," he continued to holler, as tousle-headed children began peeking from doorways. Balancing the pot with one hand he reached into his pocket for a whistle and blew. Soon the children were dancing out to meet him, followed gradually by their mothers wondering about all the racket. Cheerfully, Peter explained the merits of his crockery and led them back to his display where Metro was busy selling pots. He had hopes it was going to be another successful day.

Peter and his brother-in-law travelled together in the early years, becoming great friends and partners. When business was brisk Rupchan remained at home preparing another batch of pots, while Metro hauled a finished load to market. At other times Peter preferred to "be his own boss," peddling the crockery himself.

Hooking up a pair of mismatched oxen, one white and one red, Rupchan would plan a route encompassing the most likely towns to sell his wagonload of pottery. Occasionally he set up his display at Daschuk's livery barn in Preeceville. More frequently he marketed his wares in the surrounding villages and towns: Buchanan, Kelvington, Canora, Norquay and Kamsack, and those in between. Gradually his circuit increased, reaching the southern limits of Calder, Sheho, Yorkton and Kelliher. The Doukhobors proved to be some of his best customers. Even in later years

In the background is a wagonbox with sleighs similar to the one Rupchan used in the winter time to travel with his pots. On the right is Peter's oldest son, Nick with Mike Kudeba.

they continued to bake in the old clay ovens that were becoming less frequently used elsewhere.

Rupchan sold his pots from farm to farm, but his main destination was a populated town where sales would be plentiful. He found it an imposition when he or Metro were charged a vending fee as was occasionally the case like on February 27, 1930 at Foam Lake. The $2 rate was a relatively steep fee considering that Rupchan's pottery prices ranged from five cents for whistles to 45 cents for two gallon crocks.¹ It usually took him a week or two to sell a load of pots bringing in a total revenue of only $50 to $80.

Whenever Rupchan reached a town, he chose a place to park in the centre of the market area, tying his oxen together to graze. For sleeping he tethered them by the wagon. It became so much of a habit that the oxen, even when they were loose at home, wandered over and slept by the wagon.

Travelling by oxen was a slow process so Rupchan switched to horses in the early 1920s. He used a small team that weighed about 900 pounds apiece. One was a mare named Mary and the other a white horse named

Buster. Later he used a little stud named Indianchek. Called this by the Rupchan children, it meant "Little Indian" because the horse had been traded by the local Indians for food and other supplies.

In the summertime for short distances, the horses pulled a high wagon with wooden wheels and a double box that was divided with hay. In the winter the box was placed on a pair of long, wooden runners. In later years Metro made a hayrack out of poles with rails around the sides. It was six or seven feet wide by 12 feet long and was used to haul hay and carry the pottery.

Rupchan systematically packed his precious earthenware for each long trip. First he layered the wagon with hay and then stacked the pots in rows. Placing the bigger pots on the bottom he filled them with hay and set smaller pots inside. An 18 by 36 inch box served as the seat and was filled with toys, whistles and smaller items. Carefully he covered the load with a huge white tarpaulin.

In the towns where he stopped there was usually about a one-acre square marketing area with boards or railing built around the outside to tie horses. Here Rupchan set up his display. Taking two or three pots, he left either Metro or one of his sons sitting at the display while he ambled through the streets selling his crockery.

"He would have samples so people could pick out what they wanted and then he knew where it was packed and could find it in the hay," said John, Rupchan's third oldest son, who after he reached the age of 12 often travelled with his father.

Besides giving toys and whistles to the children, Rupchan sometimes donated his pots to those that obviously could not afford to buy one. He always had a small crowd around his wagon listening to his amazing and humorous stories, while he enticed them to buy his crockery.

As the pots were sold Rupchan threw the hay to the horses. At the end of the day the tired peddlers slept in the wagonbox with the horses tied to the wheels. A special box that fit into the wagon was made to carry their lunch, but people were generous and often they were invited in for meals.

Still Rupchan encountered many hardships along the way, the weather being one of the major culprits. Although the bulk of his travelling was done in the summertime whenever he wasn't occupied with the farm, he would sometimes venture out in late fall and early spring through winter-like conditions.

Rupchan found that riding through the snow with the wagon on runners was smoother and safer for the pots, except for one year. The snowfall had been heavy as he started travelling south towards Kelliher, but by the time he returned it had melted. He found it just a little rough going with the runners cutting into the gravel road. Luckily, as he neared home, he found there was plenty of snow again.

Bundled and wrapped against the biting winds and inclement weather, Rupchan often endured trips fighting his way through deep banks of snow. Not only was it hazardous, cold and tiring, but occasionally he encountered unexpected snowstorms and had to find a place to stay until it was over. At most the blizzards only lasted for a day or two, but in March of 1923 the roads were entirely blown in near Stenen. Luckily he was near a favourite and frequent resting place at the home of his mother's second cousin, Mike Wihnan. There he was forced to remain for three weeks.

"He couldn't move," said Bill, the son of Mike and Polly. "He was scared to get out because if the sleigh upset all the pots would break." Eventually he reached home safely. He didn't let the episode deter his future winter jaunts.

George Boychuck, one of Rupchan's sons-in-law, recalled when he was 8 or 10 years old the potter coming to their home at Lady Lake, 15 miles south of Usherville. It was in the wintertime in the 1920s and Rupchan, who was headed for home with his sleigh and horses, stayed overnight, taking refuge from the knife-like cold. Boychuck's first impressions of Peter were that he was very good-natured, very generous and friendly. He was also an inveterate story teller. "He told tales, not stories," he said.

Sometimes events in Peter's life tested his good nature. One episode occurred in the Verigin or Crooked Lake vicinity. Rupchan often traversed the lonely roads, stopping at isolated farmyards, hoping for a sale. Late one evening he heard about a wedding in progress. Although no one there needed any pots he was invited to spend the night. Rupchan was concerned about the horses sampling the hay from his wagon and breaking the pots, but he was assured the gates were closed and the horses were out. The following morning he discovered five or six horses around his wagon, and all that remained of his pottery were broken pieces in the straw.

It was beyond Rupchan how the horses could have opened the gate by themselves as the farmer so adamantly said must have happened. Upon closer inspection Peter noted the fragments were from old used pots. He had been tricked by his not-so-accommodating hosts who had stolen his new ones, then replaced them with old pieces of pots, turning their horses loose to make it appear as if the animals were the culprits. Rupchan was furious but he had no recourse.

Perhaps the strangest episode occurred sometime later as he travelled through the gently rolling hills to the south towards Buchanan. It was during this trip that he located the lost wallet and smashed his pots before returning home. What was running through his mind that day? Perhaps the sales had not been good and he felt he had been on the road long enough? It would have been sensible to take them home or sell them, but this was an unexpected windfall and equivalent earnings. Maybe he had only a few remaining pieces to sell and realized he couldn't give them away or it would cost him future business? This is all the more peculiar in light of the fact that evidence has been found of him repairing cracked pots before final firing in an effort to try and save them and either selling them or keeping them for his own use. Whatever his logic it was obvious to Safta something was peculiar. Rupchan never said a word.

The following year, when Peter's brother-in-law, Jim Safruk took a load of pots to the same area to sell, people were reluctant to buy, even angry at the salesman for trying to peddle the potter's wares. It was only then that the incident of the previous year was gradually revealed to a puzzled Safruk and the true story brought back to Usherville.

There were those that thought he had kept the money in the wallet, others that knew he hadn't thought he should have, but all seemed displeased with his actions and for having the nerve to come back and try to make some money off of them.

Unabashed, Rupchan continued on with his pottery business. Utilizing his time wisely, Peter scrounged through junkyards during his return trips home. He collected material for glazes, old sprockets and gears for making imprints in his pots and gathered discarded parts of toys to use as moulds, as well as other useful gadgets.

It was after one of these nuisance-ground forages that the children were listening for the steel wheels of the wagon scraping over the stones on the road to their farm, indicating their father's return. Instead they heard the sound of a bugle tooting several miles away. Not only had he found the horn in the dump but he magically dropped three used bicycles on the ground in front of the astonished children. Thereafter they could hear his toots long before he appeared and would race out to meet him on their bicycles.

The nuisance grounds was also handy for Rupchan in other ways. He picked up old broken pots which people had thrown away and used them "as models for designs in an attempt to determine market demand."[2] Totally isolated from other craftspeople, Rupchan was unable to discuss the conditions, problems and successes of his business. Experimentation and ideas sprouted entirely from his own wellspring of creativity without the benefit of outside stimulation. He was alone with his frustrations of earning a living and without anyone to understand his artistic temperament.

Chapter 9

PERSONAL DIFFERENCES
(1920-1930)

RUPCHAN'S ARTISTIC PURSUITS WERE THWARTED CONTINUALLY with demands on his time. He had to provide hay and feed for the cattle and cut immense amounts of firewood to heat his home and fire his kiln. Everything was a tremendous amount of back-breaking work. He also continued each autumn to walk south for the harvest season which cut into already limited intervals he spent on his pottery.

Although Rupchan found occasional excursions to market his wares an agreeable change, he became content to let Metro do most of the travelling while he remained at home creating his pottery. He wanted to spend more time at his clay work. Safta wanted him to farm. It became a contentious point between them.

To outward appearances Safta seemed satisfied with her life, devoting herself to raising their children, working hard establishing the farm and ensuring there was enough to eat. Her robust frame had increased over the years and her countenance showed the strain of the rugged conditions of her life. Yet she was equipped with extraordinary abilities in endurance and survival.

Relatively well educated compared to many in the area, Safta was able to converse in several languages. Besides her native Ukrainian she spoke Romanian better than Peter and also knew a little German from when she had taken the mandatory language in grade three in Austria. After arriving in Canada at age 11 she taught herself how to read and write English, as did

Paul, Safta, Elizabeth, Safta's mother Katrina Safruk, Jim (Metro), ca. 1924.

her brother Metro, with a little help from a preacher in Canora. Every Sunday she read the Bible as her children sat obediently around her. She was a good cook and an adept businesswoman managing the finances for the family. In short, she was the boss.

Indulgent with her visionary husband, Safta helped Peter to some extent, particularly in the early years when she had been a starry-eyed young bride; she worked at his side assisting with the initial kneading and mixing of the clay for his "important" work. But the novelty had worn off and her help gradually dwindled because of other obligations.

Although Rupchan spoke with a heavy European accent, he had an excellent command of English, but he had not had the opportunity for schooling and could neither read nor write. Nor could he count past 10. Piling his coins in stacks of 10s on the kitchen table in rows of 10, Safta would then add up the piles and extra change to arrive at the total.

The pottery income was welcome, but Safta grew steadily more impatient with Peter and his clay diversions. She began grumbling about his time being better spent managing and developing the farm into a respectable operation. At that point he was farming 25 acres, an amount adequate only to feed the livestock. She and the children took care of the cattle, milking 13 cows, while he supplied the firewood and hay. Peter seemed to be increasingly absent, either in his pottery workshop or out selling his pots. Safta wanted more practical production on the farm from her creatively-inclined, musing husband. She also wanted more help with their family that had rapidly changed and increased in numbers.

Arthur, born in 1920, had been followed by Elizabeth who arrived prematurely on the pottery studio floor in 1922. Paul appeared in 1923 and Lena in 1925. Safta's mother had married Wasyl Huschuk in August of 1920 and had moved several miles farther east of Usherville, which no doubt made it even lonelier for Safta and weighed heavily on her.

Peter was conscientious enough to continue working wherever he could to earn cash to support the family, but he was also fiercely independent. Becoming uppermost in his contemplations was the need to establish a homestead in his own name. It rankled within his chauvinistic traits to live on land owned by his wife. He was pulled apart, struggling with an internal turmoil about his future. As he contemplated his plans for locating another homestead, he continued each fall to work out at harvest time. At least it was sure money.

Agnes, Peter with Paul on his lap, Jim (Metro) and Nick, ca. 1924.

In 1925 as the honking geese flew south overhead in giant Vs, Peter walked along the railroad track to Balcarres with his neighbour, John Trehubiak, to stook and thresh for farmers along the way. Finishing work in the late fall they hiked home again, stopping on the way at John's father-in-law's. It was only then they heard the news about the death of their children. Another epidemic (perhaps diphtheria) with diarrhea complications had claimed Peter's children, Paul and Lena. John Trehubiak also had lost one child.

There had not been any way for the men to be contacted with the news, nor had there been any medical help for the children. Paul died in his brother Nick's hands. Safta had been the one to place her lifeless children on the converted democrat and haul them to the cemetery.[1] The children had been buried for almost a month before Peter returned home. The loss was devastating.

The following year Peter, with his eldest son, Nick, was once again away from home at harvest time, just four miles south of Preeceville at the Swan farm. It rained, forcing them to quit work. They walked home early on Saturday, stopping at Peter's parents' place. There they discovered Nikolai had died on Oct. 27 and had been buried on the 29th. His death, of natural causes, was unexpected and they had missed the funeral by several days.

Nikolai had been 69 years old. The staunch Romanian had never learned to speak Ukrainian. This attitude reflected the idle life he adopted after reaching the age of 60 when he declared himself retired. Akseniya kept working, but Nikolai did as he pleased, preferring at harvest time to take his namesake grandson, Nick, picking cranberries instead of putting up crops. He led a leisurely life, collecting rent from his daughter and son-in-law, Veronia and George Seminuik, who lived on Wasyl's land. He had remained disrespectful towards his wife and perhaps Akseniya was partially relieved by his death. She promptly gave Wasyl's land to Veronia.

Peter was in agreement with his mother's decision about his brother's land, but began to dread working away from home. It seemed every time he returned there was another tragedy to face. In some respects it was not worth the problems he encountered for the relative cash he earned. Payment had not improved much for harvesting work over the years.

In 1927 harvesters received only 75 cents or a dollar for a 10 hour day and they worked six days a week. Driving a team of horses earned 50 cents more a day but it was up to the team owners to look after them, which made the day 16 hours or longer. Still Peter kept at it as the family continued to grow and the income was always needed.

In the spring of 1927 another son, George, was born to Safta and Peter. Two years later in August their last child, a daughter they named Katherine (Katie) after Safta's mother, arrived on the scene. Safta had given birth to a total of 13 children, losing five (Mary, Dora, Bill, Paul and Lena) to flu and diphtheria epidemics. She felt other pangs of loss as her oldest children began leaving home to work.

Nick left at age 15 and lived with his Auntie Veronia and Uncle George Seminuik for three years. In the summer of 1926 he worked as a grade man and gave the money to his mother to pay the taxes because they were behind again. In 1927 he went to Regina to work, then returned to Usherville where he lived for three years with his Uncle Jim (Metro) helping to farm his land.

The Rupchan family about 1928 on the SW3-38-5-W2. Back: Nick. Middle Row: Art, John, Jim, Peter, Safta, Agnes. Front Row: Elizabeth, George.

In about 1928 their oldest daughter, Agnes, who was called Sarah in the school records and by some of the neighbours, quit school and went to work for Bolas Izdebski's store and post office in the newly established village of Endeavour. The money she made helped raise her siblings.[2]

The extra money provided by Nick and Agnes was a godsend, but without the help of her oldest children at home, Safta found it even harder to cope, especially as Peter was not in the least bit interested or suited to farm seriously. She was frustrated when her admonishments went unheeded by the determined potter. They began to fight more and more about Peter's pottery operation. It was time, she declared, to settle down into respectable farming and forget his pottery foolishness.

Peter began looking for a homestead sometime around 1928. Then he discovered a vacant one, two miles north on a hill. He applied for the NW10-38-5-W2 in 1929, but was refused when it was discovered another man, John Sawchuk, still had a claim on it. Rupchan's $10 entry fee was returned. Eventually Sawchuk abandoned the quarter. Peter reapplied and was accepted the following year.[3]

In the meantime the rift between Safta and Peter became wider and Rupchan's desire to own a homestead in his own name became deeper. Safta perhaps didn't understand the nature of her husband, the passion and earnestness, the fervour with which he pursued his ambitions. One big blow-up ignited when one of the youngest children fell into a tub of hot water. Peter was very upset and he blamed Safta. Shortly after this he moved to the "hill," as his quarter on the northwest of 10 came to be called.

The final clincher to keep them apart for several years came when Peter took the three boys, John, Jim and Art to help with building on his new homestead. This left no one to help Safta with the other farm. She was furious. Rupchan escaped to his retreat.

Chapter 10

NEW BEGINNINGS
(1930-1935)

P ETER FELT A SENSE OF RELIEF WHEN HE ESCAPED FROM the domineering clutches of his wife. But his self-imposed exile was not as simplistic as it first appeared. He took a long time to establish himself again and had he known what was in the future, perhaps he would not have been as enthusiastic to start over. However, fiercely independent, Peter forged ahead with his new homestead.

He chose to build his house on a hill that overlooked a steep incline to the south, about 100 yards from the edge of his quarter. When he cleared the trees away he could see two miles away to the village of Usherville and his wife's farm. To the north dense forest crowned the 300 feet deep Etoimami Valley. The North Etoimami River lying at its base wound and twisted its way to join the Pewei River and then flowed northward into the Red Deer River.

A theory has been suggested that it was along this water system that Henry Kelsey, the first European man to see the prairies, travelled.[1] Perhaps he too saw the rolling country covered with poplar and willow scrub, where the majestic spruce and tamarack gave way to muskeg and prairie grasslands. Maybe he followed the deep, rutted Indian trails that cut through the valley and rested with the natives at their two encampments situated along the north-south watershed between the Etoimami and Lilian Lakes.[2] Did he feel as Rupchan did nearly 250 years later; a freshness, a newness, a thrill of conquering unknown terrain? A new beginning?

There is no doubt, Peter was overjoyed to have another opportunity to claim a homestead in his own name. For years the loss of his former one and having to live on one in his wife's name, had irritated him like a sharp stone in his shoe. Now he had another start.

His oldest son, Nick, was then living and working with his uncle so it fell to the three younger boys, Jim, John and Art to help clear the land and build the house. It wasn't a matter of simply building a house. Each log had to be cut, peeled and shaped to fit the corners. Mudding the cracks came next. Rupchan painstakingly split spruce for the shingles of his new home as he had done for all his houses. He attached his workshop to the house, then added a small shed. Joining this was a second building that opened to the west with a doorway about 10-12 feet wide. Behind this Rupchan placed the glass crusher which he operated with a rope through the roof. The barn, pig pen and chicken coops were at the base of the hill on the north side, where two springs provided water. Here he also planted a row of six spruce trees. His buildings complete, Peter began clearing the land.

Remains of Rupchan's house on the NW10-38-5-W2, with workshop attached on the right. This view is looking up the hill to the north. The kiln was to the right. (See also photo on page 69 for more complete set of buildings.)

CROSS SECTION OF
THE KILN ON THE NW10 · 38 · 5 · W2

"He worked hard," said George Wiwcharuk, a neighbour to the east through whose land Rupchan crossed for accessibility to his own. "The bush was really thick. He cut it into cordwood, then burned the stumps. He cleared 100 acres on his place level with the ground, 25 acres here and there." One year while living on the hill he cut 100 cords of wood himself and stacked them. Earnestly working from dawn until dusk, Rupchan's work most often came to nothing. The problem was he had a quirk of changing his mind and letting what he'd cleared grow up again. He always had a new scheme planned.

Nothing seemed to freeze on the hill and Peter grew tomato plants as huge as willows. On the south slope he had an abundant crop of exceptional cucumbers. One year he had a splendid garden giving bags of produce away for miles around. He even tried growing his own tobacco, but was unsuccessful.[3]

In the meantime his pottery work had suffered. It took years of back-breaking work to finish the buildings and clear the land. He continued with his pottery business in spare moments, using the old kiln on the SW3, but was forced to quit making pottery for almost a year in the early 1930s in order to meet the homestead requirements in time.

His sales were gradually declining as people began using other types of cooking vessels. However, Rupchan planned to look for alternate outlets to sell his pots and eventually he was able to build a smaller, more sophisticated kiln on the hill that was adequate.

Peter grinding clay by hand.

Once again making use of the numerous stones found locally, he built the kiln into the side of the hill. Described by his family as "a one-room affair" with a dividing partition, Peter actually built it along the two-room, Dutch oven principle. At the south end was a small opening through which he placed the wood into a four foot chamber for the fire. At the opposite end was a bigger door that led into a larger room measuring eight feet wide by 15 feet long by eight feet deep where he stacked the pots. He built a partition wall with a circular opening that allowed the heat to pass through.[1]

His workshop was also more efficient. There was a small low door to the north where he brought in his clay and firewood to heat the shop. Two other doors were located on the south; one led outside to the kiln and the other to the interior of the house. In one corner sat the kick-wheel and in the opposite corner stood pails of glaze. Along the walls was a stove to heat the building. On the southeast side his clay was in mounds, covered by wet gunny sacks. Also inside his workshop was the box made out of planks where he worked the dirt with his bare feet.

It was about this time Peter bought his six horsepower, stationary gas engine which he used to mix and grind the clay. He had long since given up the idea of using the unreliable windmills. Modifications were needed, so pounding iron rods into the edge of a huge wooden wheel, he then fitted a chain around the circumference. Attaching the wheel to the motor he was able to slow down the engine to increase power and to run the grindwheel at the necessary slower pace.

About this time Rupchan put his ingenuity to work outfitting a wagon with buggy wheels on the front and hay rake wheels on the back. This helped keep the wagonload of pottery level when he travelled up steep inclines, particularly when he took a shorter route to his home on the hill, which ran parallel to the railroad tracks.

HANDMADE STONES FOR GRINDING
GLASS, CLAY, FLOUR

Wooden wheel Rupchan used to modify six horsepower motor to grind clay.

Peter lived in relative isolation for several years while Safta and the youngest children lived below. Even if he had wanted to he couldn't leave and risk forfeiting the right to his homestead. He stayed to develop it, trying to prove to himself and the world that he could do it. All the while he continued to work steadily at his pottery whenever the opportunity arose, even working late in the evenings trying to make extra money.

Sometimes customers appeared at his shop, but not always to buy pottery. Things were often stolen but this was reduced when Peter hung pieces of tin to rattle in the wind while he was away. For the most part people were as honest and interested in his innovative work as he was in patiently explaining his operation to them.

When the neighbourhood men were not working in the bush or farming they joined Rupchan to watch him magically transform the lumps of clay into perfectly formed pots. They would sit for hours mesmerized as Peter told stories to entertain them. His place at times became a "bachelor haven." Sometimes he tried to entice people to work with clay but most refused.

One entrepreneur, John Federuik, took advantage of Rupchan's clay works operation and experimented a little on his own. He made bricks for a chimney and took them to Peter for firing. Unfortunately Federuik's venture was unsuccessful. The bricks soon fell apart and crumbled due to the inferior clay he used.

When Peter's children were older they helped with his pottery. Besides the more laborious and tedious tasks such as preparing the clay, Nick and John made dolls and whistles. The first time John recalls is when he and his brothers were living with their father up on the hill while helping him to cut wood. One night after John had already retired and the others were sleeping, his father approached him quietly and asked him to go and make roosters and dolls. John agreed and thereafter each night sat on the end of his bunk and made them out of the same clay that his father used to make pots.

John fashioned a perogie-like shape first, then squeezed out a stem for the neck and a little bit of a tail. He said, "Father had been to the nuisance ground and found some old broken toy with nice steel. It opened in half and I put two sides around the shaped clay and it made a rooster. There was nothing to it. Dolls were easy, too. One side was flat and the other side was the face of a doll formed by a discarded toy. He found that in the nuisance ground first."

Only surviving rooster whistle available.

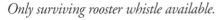

To the older children Peter's work was normal. "When you live with it and see it all the time, it just seems to be an automatic thing, just like cutting wood, just the thing you did to earn a living," observed John.

However, the younger children when they attended school were teased about their father's work and called taunting names like "horshkodry" (pottery peddler) that embarrassed them. Peter seemed oblivious to any condescension from others and continued fervently with his work.

He led a relatively quiet existence, pursuing his career, drawing from some inner strength to combat the isolation of his work in an area where he was considered anything but average. People had viewed Rupchan as eccentric from the first time they had laid eyes on him poking in the nuisance grounds, until they found him knocking on their door with pottery for sale. They knew him to be kind-hearted, hard-working and generous to a fault. Although he spent hours regaling folks with stories and anecdotes he was seemingly self-disciplined in his personal habits.

"He didn't seem to have much fun in him, no drinking, no dances, but he smoked. I never saw him drink until my wedding when he had one drink," said Nick, who married Dora Leason in 1935. Some neighbours, however, recall Rupchan inviting them to accompany him on one of his tedious all day trips to dig clay for his pottery and discovering he had brought a bottle of alcoholic refreshments along to lessen the boredom.

Peter also smoked for several years, buying Pilot tobacco for five cents a package, said John, who also formed the habit. The local store paid 10 cents for a dozen eggs and John used to steal six eggs from his mother and go to the store to buy a package of tobacco.

Peter's children generally agreed their father was not too strict. It seems Safta was the stern one and Peter the lenient of the two.

"John, Jim and Art played music when it was haying time instead of working. Dad never made them work," recalls his daughter Katie, who was often carried on her father's shoulders.

Although mostly good-natured he did have a fiery temper at times, particularly if the children didn't listen to their mother. "He threw a five-foot crowbar at me and I shut the door. It went through the door," said Nick.

Rupchan in action.

John, too, tells of a time his mother gave him a pail and asked him to go for water. He refused, then walked a little ways away, but his father had heard the discussion. "He had a hammer in his hand and it just went past me—voom!" said John. "Then I went fast and got the water after that."

Common knowledge abounds that Rupchan told people their fortunes by reading their left palms. He later admitted to his family that he was just fooling people, doing it for fun, but many took him seriously. Especially women who would bring articles of their husband's clothing and ask Peter about infidelities they suspected or other obscure questions. Peter enticed them to come again to hear more, especially when he was living alone on the hill. What he really wanted was the cooking they brought in payment for his assistance. "He was a terrible cook," explained Nick.

Peter's mystical predictions developed to where he was playing upon people's superstitions, especially when problems with the stealing of his pots increased. He generally let it be known that through his magical powers he would discover the thieves. This threat stopped the stealing for awhile. Then a rumour began that he was working with the devil and placing curses on the stolen pots which caused them to break as they were being carried away. As ridiculous as the rumour was, it put an end to the thefts completely.

However, the gossip persisted about his curses causing pots to break and was further substantiated when the earthenware he gave in payment for his debts also cracked. There was a logical basis for this foolish superstition but it wasn't the result of any supernatural arrangements. The truth was his pots did tend to break, but only because they were at times underfired. The unpredictability of the properties of his locally found clay and the unsophisticated firing techniques resulted in many problems with the durability of his pots. Some of the bigger crocks and bowls were wired on the outside to keep them together.

People's outlandish beliefs in Peter's supernatural powers didn't bother the tolerant potter, who played on their ignorance and fears. In a way he was flattered by the attention when all kinds of misfortunes that occurred in the neighbourhood began to be blamed on "Pete's Devil." The community needed something or someone to blame for all their adversities and he played along.

Nick explained, "We had a squirrel in the house that ran between the stringers. People didn't know about it. When they heard the scrabbling noise Dad said, 'There's the devil.' This only served to fuel people's imaginations, especially those who were already heavily involved with spiritual dabblings."

Séances were common long before Rupchan said he had a "devil" in him. This popular practice often revealed many predictions that later became true. A prime example was of the death of a local resident in 1919, which was predicted by the prophetic table (talking table) and that has stuck in the minds of the older people to this day.

People would gather on a stormy winter's night to play cards and drink a little homebrew. Later, around the table, they held hands. Turning down the coal oil lamps for atmosphere, they asked questions. If the table rose they knew the answer was yes to whatever their query.

"How many dollars in your pocket?" was a common ice breaker. The table tipped and knocked the answer on the floor. The séance participants claimed that this method had revealed the identity of the local cattle rustlers before the police latched onto them.

Rupchan had better things to do with his time than be involved with this silly parlour game. He was consumed with the problems of establishing his homestead and managing his pottery operation.

Chapter 11

RECONCILIATIONS
(1935-1939)

O NE OF THE DRAWBACKS OF PETER'S FARM ON THE HILL was the fact that in the winter there was too much draft so he couldn't fire his pots or they would have cracked. Living on his own wasn't easy either.

On the other hand life for Safta was far from idyllic, but she was determined to make a go of it, even though at some point in the 1930s she ran into difficulties. George, the youngest son explained: "We, on the SW of 3, were pressed by the L.I.D. (Local Improvement District), to pay taxes or else they were going to sell that quarter or they would foreclose. A cattle buyer came and Mother had to raise $10. So the cattle buyer looked at the cattle and took the best steer that we had and he gave her $9. He couldn't give her $10—she had to have another dollar. Then he took the best suckling calf we had for the other dollar. That was the $10. What happened wasn't necessary. It wasn't the government that was foreclosing. It was just the envious local secretary and he was putting the pressure on."

Safta survived that indignant crisis, suspecting that Peter was behind it hoping to force her to move. She admitted she was weakening and wished Peter was back helping her. It would be so much easier if they worked together. Besides this, the boys were getting older and bringing home friends to play music with and to party. They also would bring home two 100 pound sacks of flour, expecting her to keep one and bake bread for them with the other. She was tired of the extra work.

Peter was earnest about a reconciliation on the condition she move up to his farm. Safta realized how serious he was about staying on the "hill" as he neared completion of the requisites for his homestead. Peter proudly displayed his handiwork and showed her the wonderful home he had built for her. Finally he convinced Safta to move up to his new farm. Three of their sons, Jim, John and Art, who were older by then and able to take care of themselves, remained behind on the old homestead.

It was a bright sunny day for the Rupchan family when Peter came to collect them in the democrat. Safta and Peter rode in the buggy, while Katie, George and Elizabeth scampered ahead on foot. Every few yards the children spied shining coins lying along the trail. They fell upon them delighted. It was many years later they suspected their father had dropped the change on his way down to fetch them, hoping they would like their new home. It worked. They thought they were going to a wonderful place.

Peter thought so too, especially when he officially received his land certificate from the Province of Saskatchewan's Department of Natural Resources dated the 25th of September, 1936. He was overjoyed. He had reached his primary goal at last!

Receiving his official title helped dispel the dark cloud of the death of his mother that had occurred 10 days earlier on September 15. Her life and end was synonymous with Peter achieving his final goal. Both had worked hard, enduring strenuous setbacks and prickly opposition to their natures. Akseniya had been a feisty lady of 69 who milked cows until the day she reached her heavenly reward and Peter had fulfilled his dream of owning a homestead. Both mother and son were finally at peace with themselves.

Rupchan seemed to have found a secure niche at last. He began communicating more with the outside world, looking at different opportunities for income connected with his pottery. No longer was his profession considered peculiar. Instead his business was increasingly successful and Rupchan was commanding attention from diverse sources.

In a 1939 newspaper article written by Leo Lubiniecki he explained:[1] "The countryside buys my wares and some I take to the stores. People come from all over the province and some stop in who visit the oil wells at Kakwa.... But I would rather that some large firm (he mentioned a small mail order house) would buy them from me and then I wouldn't bother with local sales. I would just work and work."

Rupchan obviously enjoyed his pottery work and at one point had even looked seriously at the possibilities of job offers. "...Yes I had two jobs offered me. They were going to pay me $4 a day but, you know, I didn't have title to this farm. It's a homestead and I didn't want to leave for fear of losing it..."[2]

Some of these offers probably occurred when Rupchan contacted various clay companies about purchasing samples for experimentation. From Estevan he received two different batches of clay. The first shipment was good, but the second one had small stones and the pots cracked. Besides this flaw, the clay was too expensive to transport and Rupchan returned to his own "homemade" variety. While this was progressing other people became aware of his talents.

Indications point to a job proposal in Saskatoon. It seems unlikely that the offer came through the University in Saskatoon, according to James Cameron Worcester, whose father ran the one-man ceramic engineering department from 1921 onwards. Perhaps it was Dr. George Ernest Dragan, who at some point mentioned he would try and get Peter a job in Saskatoon.

Rupchan first came in contact with Dr. Dragan during election time one year. Rupchan's son, Nick, then 19 years old, was sent to vote at Wadena as a delegate on behalf of the Usherville district from township 38. Dragan, a doctor from Saskatoon, was one of the first Ukrainian political delegates to run in an election. Dragan introduced himself and asked Nick questions about his life at Usherville and was amazed to learn about Peter's pottery enterprise.

Time passed. Dragan was elected as the Liberal MLA in the Kelvington riding between 1934 and 1938. Upon investigation Dragan discovered there was no information on Rupchan's work recorded at the University in Saskatoon. On June 24, 1937 while in the Usherville district he paid Rupchan a visit.

Wes Hawkins, a resident of Endeavour guided Dragan to the Rupchan homestead across staunch Conservative George Wiwcharuk's land for fear

Dr. Dragan visited Rupchan on the NW10-38-5-W2 on June 24, 1937.

there would be a political confrontation. The youngest children were at school and missed the prominent visitor but a photograph taken by Hawkins recorded the event. Dragan made notes of Peter's primitive operation and took samples of his pottery back to Saskatoon.

Dr. Dragan's wife, Rose, was heavily involved in the Saskatoon Arts and Crafts Society and there is evidence she may have placed some of Rupchan's pottery on display at a showing for the society in approximately 1939, after her husband's visit.[3] In subsequent dealings it has been suggested Dragan may have also tried to persuade Rupchan to purchase some glazes he brought from Saskatoon but Peter declined because they were too expensive. It is thought Dragan relented and eventually gave him some.

Not long after Dragan's visit Rupchan encountered problems with his pottery clay that brought about an entirely different aspect to his methods of earning money.

Lubiniecki wrote in his June 24, 1939 article in the Regina *Leader-Post* that he and Rupchan discussed the qualities of clay found on the potter's farm:[4]

[Rupchan said.] "I told you one of its chief weaknesses was that it dried so quick in the kiln that it would burn. Then when you picked the vessel up the part you held it by would break in your hand."

"I wandered to the other end of the farm and dug at the base of a large hill there, something like the hill on which this house and workshop stands. I found clay. I expected to. There is so much around here but I dug farther and found a heavy shiny substance in the clay..."

"Coal?"

"No. Lead! I melted it at home and sold it to stores and to blacksmiths. Then I sent some away through a storekeeper. It was tested at Regina and they said it was a good sample of lead with traces of silver, zinc, copper and nickel. A Regina syndicate has an option on the farm now. I'm to get a $1000 when they start work and a little out of every ton of metal that they mine. They trenched around the hill and took samples but haven't done any more work on it."

At the end of Lubiniecki's article he speculated that, "perhaps little by little the potter's workshop on the hill will be known far and wide and Peter Rupchan will be mentioned as the potter who went to search for clay and found a mine."

Peter never found a mine but there is little doubt that he discovered lead in some of his clay. Nick said that his father had located a good source of clay about 50 feet north behind the house on the hill. A 20 foot hole indicated this was where he took most of his clay. This was also supposed to be where the lead was found. According to Norman Harris, when Peter made and baked the pots using this clay, part of them would melt out from lead. Rupchan may have used this obstacle to his advantage, however, there does not seem to be any official verification of any large amounts of lead in the soil.

It is common family knowledge that Rupchan fabricated a ruse by melting battery lead that he shipped to a firm in Regina telling them it was collected from his soil. He had decided eking out a living on the homestead was unacceptable. He wanted to sell out and take a job for the consistent income it would provide. His ploy snagged several groups of interested people.

As early as 1932 some unidentified person held a surface lease on land in the district and in 1934 Petro Engineering did some work in the area. W.J. Sanderson held a surface quartz claim on Rupchan's quarter (NW10) in 1937. Ed Doyle, a building contractor from Sturgis, also had some connection with prospecting on Rupchan's land, perhaps in association with

Sanderson. Both men most likely worked for or represented a company. Doyle apparently went through an office in Regina to lay a claim on section 10 (including Rupchan's quarter) so no one else could touch it, pounding in his claim stakes across the property. There is also the possibility that Doyle might have had some association with some people by the name of Lee who came from the United States.[5]

The Lees arrived in a stationwagon between 1937-39 sometime before the second world war broke out. Mr. Lee and a partner from Minnesota came together the first time to analyze the situation. The second time Lee's wife also came along and they brought a tent, camping out for a month beside the North Etoimami Lake.

Among their provisions they included some clothing for the Rupchan family. The youngest son, George, was given a pair of shoes; it was the first time he'd ever worn leather footwear. Before that he always wore runners. For Peter they brought samples of clay, glazes and two augers; one was a telescopic pipe variety that could be extended, the other was a solid rod. Both were to be used so Rupchan could dig deeper for clay.

Because of Ed Doyle's claim on Rupchan's home quarter, the Lees couldn't work it, but did so on the ones close by like the southeast of 15 and 22. Part of these workings happened to be a claim that Rupchan himself took out on June 17,1937. (He claimed a Legal Sub-Division, or L.S.D., off section 15.) The Lees found just chunks and pieces of lead and perhaps some type of iron ore while checking for lead and minerals. They had rigs to dig deep but found the lead just four inches from the surface and nothing underneath. They said there was lots of iron but it was too costly to proceed.

Rupchan's son John said that when there was supposed to be lead in the land, truck loads of dirt were hauled to boxcars and shipped for analysis, but nothing of value was found. The land was closed off sometime in 1937. Although it was decided the land was worthless, the little markers were left all over the place, some of which remain. In the meantime Peter dreamed up another ploy in an effort to make it appear his land was valuable.

The Coal Gate Oils Limited, 44 Western Trust Building, Regina, Saskatchewan, represented by Perry L. Withers, 405 Marlborough Hotel, Winnipeg, Manitoba, wrote to Rupchan on March 26, 1938. He informed

Rupchan that he planned to come soon to look into the oil the potter found while digging a water well. Although it is impossible to tell what happened exactly it seems either this company or another came to investigate. They dug a few trenches behind his property and Peter, to continue the deceit, would sneak out at night and pour oil into the trenches and holes that were dug. He was quite anxious for them to buy, but this attempt, too, failed and fizzled out.

All of Rupchan's schemes for selling his land fell through and he had to face the fact that his life on the hill wasn't as wonderful as he first anticipated. The NW of 10 turned out to be extremely windy and besides causing problems with the pottery, was almost a daily annoyance. The location was a problem for Safta who was a hefty woman by now. She had a difficult time drawing water from the well at the bottom of the steep hill and carrying it back up to the house. She found it exhausting, particularly on a hot summer day. It was also two miles farther for the children to go to school, although they did have their trusty horse, Indianchek, to rely on.

"The horse was almost human, he never would have left me," recalls Katie, the youngest daughter. He liked to lie down in the water, though, during hot days. In the winter time they went to school in a toboggan fitted with sides for holding a quilt and food. One time while going down the hill, the sleigh hit the horse in the back of the legs and the whole thing upset.

Problems like these suggested to the Rupchans that a move back down to Safta's quarter was inevitable. It wasn't an easy decision for Peter in some respects. He was well established where he was, looking forward to selling his crockery to wholesalers and wanting nothing except to continue working on his pottery. It was obviously still his main interest and an important source of income to him, although the market and methods of sales were changing.

His youngest son, George, recalls the common occurrence of travelling with his father in a wooden wagon to Preeceville when they delivered a can of cream and sold pots. On one occasion George remembered his sister Elizabeth wanted a permanent for her hair so her dad had to earn some money for it. At that time he was charging 15 cents for a flower pot. They took the usual can of cream and a few pots to sell and stayed overnight because they had to wait for Elizabeth to have her hair done. Local sales and travelling with his wares had dwindled considerably, but Peter was still enthusiastic about his craft.

Metro, finding himself temporarily out of a travelling salesman job, opened a store on another quarter he purchased farther east of his first. He began investigating other ventures, besides farming.

Peter, in the meantime, obligingly conceded to a move back to Safta's quarter now that he was securely established with his own on the hill. He decided it would be safe to leave it and build a new home for Safta where they would eventually retire.

Chapter 12

ECHOES
(1939-1944)

PETER'S RESOLUTION TO BUILD A NEW HOUSE WAS NOT AN easy decision. This would be his sixth since moving to that area of Saskatchewan. Each time constructing buildings and establishing a farmyard was a lengthy project that took several years. He had to place his pottery crafting on hold, returning to it only in spare moments or late in the evenings.

For some unknown reason this time, the 56-year-old potter gave up making pots entirely for several years. Reaching some internal decision, Peter indicated to his family that he had given up pursuing his artistic abilities and instead would farm in the future. His sudden change of heart and total acquiescence to Safta's demands was uncharacteristic, yet, admittedly life was more harmonious for the family. At least for a time.

Choosing a site carefully on a slight rise, Peter began with zeal to build a well-planned house. None of Rupchan's homes had been built in the standard Ukrainian style, nor was this one. A typical Ukrainian house faced south with the east side in line with the north star. Usually most of the windows and doors also opened to the south with one window on each end. There were none on the north. A peetch, sitting in one room for baking and heating the home, instead of having a chimney to the exterior, was vented to the attic (if the roof was thatched) from where the smoke seeped outside, providing a logical place to smoke fish. Consistent with his eccentric nature Peter used little of these traditional features for his home. He firmly faced his house east.

Beginning the house in 1939, Rupchan barely finished before the wedding of his daughter, Elizabeth, to George Boychuk, took place in it in mid 1940. Boychuk, who lived about 15 miles to the south near Lady Lake, had earnestly courted Elizabeth for three years travelling by bicycle and horseback. Rupchan had occasionally stayed overnight with the Boychuck family on his pottery selling sojourns and he knew George well. The newlyweds lived in the Rupchan's older first house in the yard on the SW of 3 for two or three years. John married in 1943 and moved into the vacated house on the "hill."

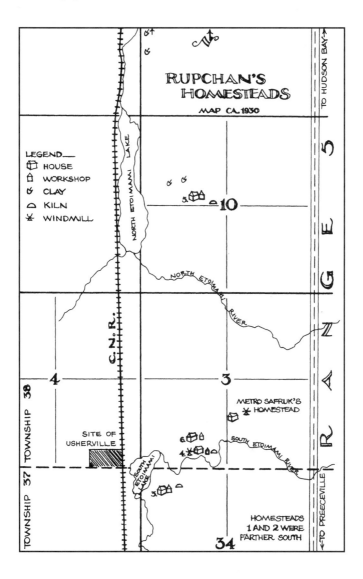

RUPCHAN'S
HOMESTEADS
MAP CA. 1930

LEGEND
🏠 HOUSE
🏚 WORKSHOP
Ⴓ CLAY
⌂ KILN
✳ WINDMILL

TO HUDSON BAY →

NORTH ETOIMAMI LAKE

NORTH ETOIMAMI RIVER

C.N.R.

5

E

G

N

A

R

Z

TOWNSHIP 38 | TOWNSHIP 37

4

3

METRO SAFRUK'S
✳ HOMESTEAD

SITE OF
USHERVILLE

SOUTH ETOIMAMI LAKE

SOUTH ETOIMAMI RIVER

← TO PREECEVILLE

34

HOMESTEADS
1 AND 2 WERE
FARTHER SOUTH

The remains of Rupchan's last house on the SW3-38-5-W2.

During the early 1940s Rupchan farmed and cut cordwood to earn a living in between construction of the outbuildings and establishing the farm. Otherwise the family survived with the ingenuity of Safta's great vitality and enormous physical endurance. She was a survivor, managing stock, chickens, pigs and a huge garden from which she sold produce, eggs, milk, cream, and meat to bring in a cash income.

At the beginning of 1944 Safta's mother, Katrina Huschuk (Safruk), passed away quietly in her daughter's home at the age of 81. She had suffered injuries four years previously after being trampled by a bull. An exceptional woman, Katrina had been keenly interested in everything from gardening to mechanics, and was dearly missed by her daughter. Already distressed, Safta became even more disturbed when Peter showed signs of resuming his pottery business.

Peter couldn't deny his creative urges any longer. Perhaps he had never entirely given them up, choosing instead to stop his pottery work for several years only so that establishing the farm would be accelerated and he could go back to his pottery business without conflicts. Possibly he never expected resettling to take so long.

By 1944, with most of the outbuildings completed, he began to erect another workshop and asked his own and neighbouring children, to pick up pails of quartz stones and glass for his glazes. He was going to return to his cherished pottery crafting.

On the quiet, still morning of Monday, July 17 in 1944 Rupchan walked to George Wiwcharuk's farm on an errand, but his neighbour wasn't home. He continued two miles north to the forestry where his sons Art, George and George Leason were cutting pulp wood. He decided to lend a hand. Two of the men sawed the trees with a Swede saw while industriously Peter peeled logs.

He was bent over at his task when the tree fellers yelled, "Tree falling!"

"All right, all right," Peter quickly answered. As he turned and ran, he stumbled and fell. The top of the tree crashed across him. The sound reverberated throughout the forest. Peter lay still. It was 1:30 in the afternoon. The police were phoned about the accident and the news of Rupchan's death travelled fast.

Apparently Peter had a tooth pulled the day before and perhaps wasn't feeling quite right, nor thinking properly. He may have misjudged things going on around him and ran the wrong direction from the falling tree. Whatever the reason, the great potter's hands were stilled forever.

His body was stored in the icehouse at his home where candles were lit and a vigil was kept day and night.

The priest from Canora performed the funeral prayers in the house three days later. Placing his body on a wagon, the entourage travelled to the cemetery, stopping at every crossroads to perform the traditional ceremony common to the Greek Orthodox rituals. He was buried in the Grichese Olentalisze Cemetery on NW22-37-5-W2, near Endeavour.[1] Forty days later, as is still the tradition, meals were cooked and offerings of fruit made to the church in honor of Peter Rupchan.

Some said he had a premonition of his death, once mentioning to a neighbour he would never live to see his buildings finished. And he hadn't. The workshop was left incomplete as were the preparations for beginning his new pottery operation.

Rupchan's funeral. He died on July 17, 1944.

Rupchan died in the same obscurity as he had been born. His death echoed his life: an untimely end begot from an untimely beginning. Clearly, Rupchan had been born 80 years or more before his time. Looking at photographs of him at work, one can see he would easily have fit in as a potter in the present day. It is a certainty selling his pottery would have been easier and there is little doubt he would have become a well-known artist. As it was, he was all but forgotten except by a select few.

His work, however, lived on long after his death, but not before it first faded into obscurity for almost 30 years. It was brought to light again in the 1970s with the writings and research of Laddie Martinosky from Gerald, Saskatchewan, and Robert Bozak of London, Ontario.

Rupchan's headstone made by Metro Safruk. (Note wrong year of birth.)

In 1969 Mr. Martinosky read a paper to the Saskatchewan History and Folklore Society in Yorkton on "Early Pottery in Saskatchewan," that featured Peter Rupchan and his work. It was subsequently published in *The Western Producer* in February of 1970. He stated, "...Much credit goes to this pioneer for his accomplishments."

Another researcher in the early 1970s, Robert M. Bozak from London, Ontario, implored others to preserve Rupchan's work and surroundings. In a letter he wrote to the Mohyla Institute in Saskatoon on June 3, 1972 he stated:

"The first thing to be recognized is the value of Rupchan's activities to the Ukrainian community and to the total history of pottery in this country. Rupchan and his work are unique when looked at in terms of other pottery activity. Most of the pottery in Canada had a very heavy influence from England, France and Germany and attempted to compete with English and French imports. Most of these potteries were in areas of considerable population and easy accessibility. They also had access to materials and to some degree equipment and probably most important of all, they were aware of each other and could at times share information. Although Rupchan was working considerably later than other potteries or potters that were making primarily hand-made ware, he was working in virtual isolation in a relatively northern portion of the province and it wasn't until near the end of his life that he had access to any processed ceramic materials. Where most potters did not have to travel far to a market, Rupchan and/or Safruk travelled as far as 120 miles one way selling pottery along the way. When this importance can be fully realized and knowing the information is obtainable, it then becomes a pressing matter.... I have become more convinced that some well thought action must be taken to guarantee that information about Rupchan's activity as a potter be made available for recording. It is very important that his pottery not become a precious commodity although in some respects it very certainly is.... Any investigation should be handled in as quiet a way as possible."

Bozak's wishes for quiet handling were denied but in some ways this turned out positively.

Rupchan's pottery pieces quickly became collectors items commanding $200 to $400 apiece. Art and antique collectors, museum curators, art gallery owners, and private collectors headed by such people as Garry Essar, Chuck Sutyla, Lindsay Anderson, Dick Spafford, John McGowan, Susan Whitney, George Chopping, and others, all had a hand in stirring up interest in Rupchan's work. They passed on their enthusiasm, sparking interest when they approached the Saskatchewan Government in 1980 about preserving a collection of 19 pieces of Rupchan's pottery as prime material examples of an ethnic community and the works of an early craftsman. Under Attorney General Roy Romanow, through the Department of Culture and Youth, the collection was purchased from the Susan Whitney Gallery for $4,750.00.

On Saturday, January 17, 1981 the collection was presented by Mr. Romanow to the Ukrainian Museum of Canada in Saskatoon. The Minister outlined the provincial historic and cultural significance of the collection stating, "Rupchan embodied the spirit of pioneer Saskatchewan and that is why we are paying tribute to him. He was creative, resourceful, persistent

Display of some of Rupchan's pottery held by the Ukrainian Museum of Canada in Saskatoon.

,and above all, independent. The products of his labours were of the style and function that he learned in Ukraine. But they are uniquely Ukrainian-Canadian."

Peter Rupchan, Ukrainian and Canadian, indeed had been independent. Although totally isolated from other craftspeople and without the benefit of proper materials he utilized his ingenuity. Inventing the equipment needed, he created thousands of utilitarian pieces of pottery. He directed his well-practised hands, drawing from some inner strength, to persevere in his ambitions, never expecting celebrity status. As he travelled and sold his pieces for a meager five to 35 cents, he could not have realized the outpourings of his creativity would ultimately result in posthumous fame. During Rupchan's humble life and untimely end he was just another pioneer trying to survive.

Epilogue

FINAL ENDINGS
(1944-1982)

F OR SAFTA, THE DEATH OF HER MOTHER AND HER HUSBAND
had been a double blow, but she rallied and remained in her home
until about 1948. Then her youngest son, George, built her a modest
new home in the hamlet of Usherville. By this time three of her middle sons
had married; John in 1943 to Annie Strelic, Jim in 1944 to Margaret Smith
and Art in 1947 to Lillian Johnson. Safta donated an acre of the SW of 3 to
the Anglican Church in approximately 1949, the same year as her youngest
daughter Katie's wedding to Mike Prestayko. In 1950 George married Helen
Trach and they moved into the last home Peter had built on the SW of 3.
Safta remained living in Usherville until her death on September 10, 1968.

Metro (Jim) Safruk sadly missed his business partner and brother-in-
law, and without Peter's pottery business he had to find other methods for
supplementing his farming income. In many respects Metro had been as
eccentric as Peter, developing windmills for cutting wood and other serv-
iceable inventions. For 15 years he owned a second quarter of land four miles
east of Usherville and a half mile south from where he operated his store.
He lost or had to sell the land for taxes in the 1930s. For a while Metro sold
fenceposts, then sometime between 1948 and 1953 he ordered a book from
a cement company in Montreal. Soon he was interested in another enterprise—making headstones.

In one week Metro built his own wooden forms for the traditionally
shaped Greek Orthodox crosses using small pieces of lumber. Then with

Metro Safruk in front of samples of his headstones.

clean, dirtless sand, he mixed the cement and poured it into the forms. He kept the concrete wet approximately two weeks to help the crosses stay strong. Although he tried chiselling in the names and dates he found it too slow. Then he discovered printing the names in while the cement was still soft worked well. For advertising purposes Metro took photographs of the intricate crosses, put prices at the bottom of the picture, then mailed them out to people. The prices ranged from eight to 14 dollars apiece and he sold them throughout the district.

"His crosses should last forever," predicts one of his nephews. Metro found if they hadn't cracked while being made they would never crack. Today, nearly 40 years later people caring for the various cemeteries throughout the area have only had to whitewash the crosses, printing over the figures with black paint where sometimes the inscriptions have faded, but otherwise they are still standing proudly erect and in sturdy condition.

Metro continued making headstones for many years, including one for his old friend and confidant, Peter Rupchan. Metro died, a bachelor, on January 20,1982.

In the early 1960s George Rupchan demolished his father's first set of dilapidated buildings, including the kiln, and worked up the field on the SW of 3. Shards of the pottery remain scattered throughout his field. The buildings and kiln on the NW quarter of 10, long since abandoned, have fallen into irreparable decay, as have Rupchan's final house and outbuildings.

Although Peter Rupchan's sons, Nick and John, made dolls, whistles and toys, and John accomplished some pots, none of his offspring ever took up pottery making as a living. The younger ones, especially, had been teased and ridiculed by insensitive classmates about their father's method of income. These feelings carried through to their adult lives causing them to become apologetic about their father's work and in later years they discarded most of his pots. Even the family members who were not affected by the condescension of others looked on his work apathetically. Making pottery was just something he did and something they were accustomed to all their lives. There was no special attachment.

Now, with the growing attention of others to Peter Rupchan's work, his family are openly sharing their pride in his accomplishments. He was a truly inspiring man, who overcame all odds and hardships to operate a successful cottage industry.

Display of Rupchan's pottery in Lindsay Anderson's collection.

Appendix 1

CHAPTER NOTES

CHAPTER 1

1. Peter Rupchan's birth certificate notes the dates June 17/29, 1883 as the day he was born. June 17 is according to the Julian calendar that was followed until 1918 in Ukraine, and the 29th refers to our present day Gregorian calendar. The 17th is the date Rupchan himself used, even after his immigration to Canada.

2. Although there is no doubt Peter was born illegitimately when his mother was 16 years old, there is no indication who was his natural father. Akseniya was still single when she married Nikolai Rupchan at the age of 18, according to their marriage certificate. Besides this, there is other evidence that suggests Nikolai was Peter's stepfather. (Refer to #4 below.)

3. a) A morge is .63 of an acres. 160 morge equal 100.8 acres.

   b) morge pronounced more/ge ...the "e" like in set; singular is morg in the Slavic language. (Morgen is the Prussian form.)

4. There are discrepancies about whether Peter began as a blacksmith or not when he was first sent away from home. Although Peter's remaining offspring don't seem to know anything about him beginning as a blacksmith, notes taken from an interview before his brother-in-law, Metro Safruk, died in 1982, still exist. He said Peter and his stepfather (Nikolai Rupchan) didn't get along. "He not liked to stay at this (blacksmith) so he ran away to learn pottery. He was a polished potter when he came to Canada," Safruk said.

CHAPTER 2

1. This was on section 34-26-31-W1.
2. Today two of these quarters have reverted back to Crown Land. They are congested with ponds, sloughs and stretches of gravelly soil. Perhaps the eventual owners between then and now found the land as worthless and unproductive as the Rupchans. (Land description: Section 18-36-5-W2.)
3. A shevek is an embroidered piece of cloth that is a special Ukrainian custom that a girl gives her beau on their wedding day.
4. The koshek Safta wore took the place of a crown used in a church ceremony. It had a ribbon or string with money sewn on it for prosperity;

CHAPTER 3

1. This is found in a personal account of Skutelnik's in "Past Endeavours: A History of Bear, Beaver Bank, Cheremosz, Endeavour, Lilian, Lilian Rural, Midland, Peerless, Rockford, Stoney Acre, Usherville, Veterans," 1989, page 434.
2. Wasyl Rupchan had industriously cleared and seeded 43 acres of land and five years earlier had established a suitable dwelling. His estate, administered by The Standard Trust Company, of the city of Winnipeg, was transferred to their office in Saskatoon. Nikolai took over the land and after 14 years it was placed in his name at a value of $1,000. When he died the land was acquired by Wasyl's sister, Veronia and her husband George Seminuik, who had been renting it.
3. a) Heating the pots then covering them with dirt is considered a very early method of firing pots.
   b) John Kudeba, who moved from the Usherville area to Canora in 1914, recalls before he left that Rupchan was already making small batches of pottery to sell locally by that time, although he was not yet travelling with his wares. Rupchan was using at least a partially built stone kiln to fire his pots. Family members, who would have been extremely young at the time, can't recall this.

CHAPTER 4

1. The Usherville post office was first located 1½ miles south of present day Endeavour from 1911-1914. It was then moved north near the present site of Usherville, while the first site became known as Annette post office and after several moves was then renamed Endeavour in 1928 when the railway went through.
2. Taken from "Past Endeavours," 1989, page 497.
3. See "Past Endeavours," pages 33-35, an article written by Norman Harris, titled "Homebrew Story" for more intensive reading on illicit homebrew making in northeastern Saskatchewan.
4. Although the family members are too young to recall when their father began doing his pottery they do remember he had built a studio with shelves and other related articles on the farm he lost. However, they felt he hadn't started his operation until sometime after 1916 when he moved and rebuilt. Various neighbours at the time insist that he began his pottery work sometime between 1910 and 1914. See Chapter 3 notes, #3 b) for further explanation.

CHAPTER 5

1. A mortgage had been registered against the land for the amount of $307 by the Toronto Dominion Bank in July of 1914. When the land was forfeited someone named Bruce McKenzie bought it for $1 in May of 1916. It was worth $1,000 according to the title. The land transfer signing over possession from Peter and Safta Rupchan to Bruce McKenzie was witnessed by James Fraser, who was a Justice of the Peace in Preeceville and also a secretary-treasurer for the town council. Then this was cancelled and Fraser himself purchased the land on June 30, 1916. An $800 value was placed on the land according to the certificate of title. This was cancelled and a new title issued to Carol Gogol on August 8, 1916.

CHAPTER 6

1. a) Temper is commonly called "grog" by potters.

b) From Joan Kanigan's thesis pages 21 and 22: "...He found a good source of clay on the banks of Etoimami Lake (Map 3). Clay samples taken from this area near his second kiln show the clay to be relatively fine and free of inclusions. These clay samples contain sand which acts as a natural temper making the clay useable without much extra work." According to Norma Harris, "this clay had too much sand. The vessels, especially if under-fired tended to crumble, because of a lack of clay to act as glue."

c) "Temper," as defined by archaeologists, is a non-plastic material that is added to clay to make it more porous and to help reduce thermal shock. Temper helps to reduce shrinkage and allows trapped moisture to escape, reducing the chances of a vessel breaking during firing. Temper can consist of almost any type of material from volcanic ash to crushed shell. Temper is very important in the construction of pottery. The kind and amount of temper used is dependent on the clay, the methods of firing and the knowledge and competency of the potter." (pp. 50-51)

2. An excerpt from Leo Lubiniecki's article in the Regina *Leader-Post*, June 24, 1939.

3. Joan Kanigan's thesis, page 24: "At the leather-hard stage a vessel will maintain its shape but its surface is pliable enough to impress or carve."

4. Ibid, pages 66-67: "The condition of the sherds roughly represents the firing conditions. Approximately 50% of the sherds in the sample were not fired adequately. This was determined by testing the sherds for the presence of calcium carbonate. About half of this 50% were obviously under fired because the sherds still contained $CaCO_2$."

5. Ibid, page 25.

CHAPTER 7

1. Professor Worcester, considered Canada's foremost authority on ceramics at that time, opened the first college of ceramic engineering at the

University of Saskatchewan in Saskatoon in 1921. It was also the first in Canada and the first in the British Commonwealth.

2. It was thought Rupchan gathered iron oxide at PeePaw Lake, however, iron oxide is commonly known as rust and it could be collected around old farm machinery. Therefore it is possible he collected a different substance at PeePaw Lake.

3. a) Worcester in a second letter said: "It is possible he could have been sent some glazes but that is pure speculation. I am quite sure he was quite familiar with the process of pulverizing glass to make glaze. Sewer pipe companies have used common salt for years as a very effective and attractive glaze."

b) One source recalls their father purchasing a pot from Rupchan in 1922 and it was definitely glazed inside with designs on the outside so he was using glazes early in his pottery career.

c) For more comprehensive information on Rupchan's glazing techniques see Appendix 1.

CHAPTER 8

1. From Joan Kanigan's thesis pages 26-27:
prices of various wares
Whistles "chickens or roosters" . . . . .$.05
Flower pots small . . . . $.15
large . . . .$.20
Makitras . . . .$.35
2 gallon pots . . . .$.45
2. Quote from Joan Kanigan's thesis, page 27

CHAPTER 9

1. When the wheels of the democrat owned by the Rupchans broke, Peter simply took them off and put hay rake wheels on it. After this time the democrat was seldom needed and Safta apparently made the comment

that "the buggy was just for funerals," because she used it when burying her children.

2. In 1930 Agnes went to work in Canora, where she met and married Bill Cheredaryk. They lived four miles east of Usherville and after a tragic fire where they lost everything they moved to Endeavour. There Agnes opened a café and Bill secured a job on the railway. They moved to Manitoba, then to St. Catharines, Ontario where they remained with their three daughters.

3. According to land title papers and letters Rupchan applied for the NW10 in August 1930, however James Cameron Worcester said Rupchan was firmly established on his farm (the SW3 near Usherville) when he and his father visited so Rupchan hadn't yet moved to the NW10.

Chapter 10

1. a) This theory was presented by Dr. Allen Ronaghen and appears as "Kelsey's Journal of 1691 Reconsidered" in "Saskatchewan History" Volume xxxvii, No.1, Winter, 1984.

b) It was along this same valley basin that the railway was constructed in approximately 1928.

2. Ironically this spot was on the southwest corner of Safta's quarter, close to the hamlet of Usherville.

3. Rupchan was able to give up smoking in approximately 1939 by chewing on candies he carried in his pockets for a year afterwards, according to some of his family members.

4. a) From Joan Kanigan's thesis page 25: "This kiln was built into the side of a hill and part of it is still intact (1989), even though it is almost completely buried. The measurements of the room that is still intact are 3.4 m long, 2.5 m deep and 2.3 m wide. This is the area where the vessels were stacked when they were fired...."

b) From the article written by Laddie Martinosky in *The Western Producer* in 1970, who may have actually seen and measured it: "...the baking section measured 10' x 8' x 6'. Adjoining it was the 6' x 6' x 6' fire chamber..."

CHAPTER 11

1. From an article written by Leo Lubiniecki for *The Preeceville Progress* on November 15, 1939, entitled "A Saskatchewan Potter."
2. Ibid.
3. Extracted from file folder F on Articles and Speeches from The Saskatoon Arts and Crafts Society (held by the Sask. Archives Board in Saskatoon) was the following:

Pottery pictures of jars and dishes which had been made by a Russian man living in Saskatchewan shown. He made his own wheel, built his own stone oven and used clay from his own farm.
[signed] Mrs. V. Morton
Feb. 1931

There seems little doubt they were speaking of Peter Rupchan in the above quotation. It is interesting to note the date is much earlier than any previously determined for Peter having had contact with the outside world. Dr. Dragan may have visited Rupchan earlier than is recorded, which is quite possible because Rupchan's son Nick was in Wadena at the political conference in about 1928 and they discussed the pottery operation there. Or perhaps Professor Worcester put Mrs. Dragan in contact with Rupchan after his visit in 1930 and she had Rupchan send some of his pots for display. Photographs remain of this event but it is impossible to tell if Rupchan's work is among them.
4. Quote from Leo Lubiniecki's article same as #1 above.
5. L. W. Lee had a claim near Choiceland, at Kelsey Lake, about this time. This may have been the same man.

CHAPTER 12

1. This is on the Aaron and Norman Harris farm, near Endeavour (NW ¼-22-37-5-W2).

Appendix 2

CONCLUSIONS OF THE SPECIALISTS

"PETER RUPCHAN WAS ONE OF THE GREATEST POTTERS IN early Saskatchewan," said Ralph Jarotski, an art teacher at Canora, who is familiar with his work. "He was a genius in his own time. Although the pottery had practical value only at that time, and wasn't regarded as art, they are pieces of art. He never signed his work but his pottery had certain characteristics, just like a signature. I would recognize it anywhere."

Part of these characteristics were born out of Rupchan's necessity of having to use whatever materials were at hand, such as digging his own clay, building his stone kiln, using old gears, sprockets and watch bearings to incise grooves in the pots, and crushing glass for glazes. These improvisations didn't always work as planned.

This becomes apparent when one examines his pottery and takes a closer look at his firing and glazing techniques. Joan Kanigan, an anthropology student from Regina, researched Rupchan's work and explains his processes more thoroughly in her thesis, excerpts of which appear occasionally in this section (in quotations, with the page numbers following).

After Peter Rupchan prepared large batches of clay he used it for all vessel types. There is little doubt he "was an accomplished potter in terms of construction technique" (page 69). Working relatively full-time, he "sold his wares in the surrounding community, and was affected by the people's choice in material, style and vessel types," wrote Kanigan. On the other

94

hand, "because he worked alone, he was not heavily influenced by market factors or peer pressure.

"It is interesting to note that although Peter Rupchan was formally trained he did not seem to exhibit a great deal of understanding about the use and properties of clay. Despite these facts, Peter Rupchan was a good potter, producing basic utilitarian wares for local use" (page 75).

One must also keep in mind the distinct possibility that Rupchan may have understood the physical properties of clay, but simply did not find any better clays to work with and could not generate high enough temperatures in his kiln.

Professional potters, Wendy Parsons and Zach Dietrich from Moose Jaw, tested a sample of Rupchan's clay from one of his last sources in the Etoimami Valley. "The first firing was a bisque using cone 6. It turned a lovely shade of red," said Parsons. They concluded Rupchan made his pottery from a low-fire earthenware clay. His aim was to low-fire the pieces to red heat around 1000-1200 degrees celsius. Although he had good throwing and working clay, he just didn't do the firing right. Perhaps this was because the design of his kiln wasn't quite adequate to insure reaching the high degree of temperature he needed. This problem might have been rectified if he had been able to buy proper fire brick from the Claybank area that were available at that time, said Dietrich. In any event he was an excellent potter with "beautiful designs."

Extensive testing of his finished products by Kanigan concurs that the temperatures required for proper firing may not always have been reached. "When pottery is fired above 1000 degrees the calcium carbonate which is sometimes in the clay, reacts with silica in the clay to form calcium silicates. This substance is stable and will not break down with time...When fired to temperatures of less than 1000 degrees the calcium oxide rehydrates, causing cracks or creating small pock marks in the surface. When tested it was found 50% of the sherds [Rupchan's] were not fired adequately," Kanigan wrote (page 66-67).

Rupchan was not aware at what temperatures he was firing his pottery until Professor Worcester visited him in August of 1930. He gave Rupchan some cones for testing the temperature, but this was only a temporary measure and Rupchan returned to using his eyes for gauging the appropriate heat. He had no other way of determining on a constant basis the temperature he needed to properly fire the clay.

The Dutch-oven style of Peter Rupchan's kiln was not effective to maintain heat. Being fairly open, it allowed oxygen into the kiln and around the vessels. Because of this oxidizing atmosphere he would not have been able "to control his firings to achieve various paste (clay or body) colours" (page 55). However, there are indications he tried other types of clays.

Towards the end of his career Rupchan experimented with kaolin, a fine white clay used in the manufacture of porcelain. Kanigan found a sample inside his last kiln that was completely unvitrified. "If it was kaolin, it would require significantly higher temperatures, 1050 degrees to 1100 degrees C to vitrify. These temperatures could not be achieved in Rupchan's kiln. The presence of this piece indicates that Rupchan was perhaps experimenting with some commercial clays" (pages 46-47).

He also had problems with his glazes. "The condition of Rupchan's glazes suggest that he was not always able to refire the wares to a sufficient temperature to properly vitrify the glass... The unvitrified glazes are determined by their bubbled nature and by the lack of a deep surface gloss..." (page 60).

He would have been familiar with the low-fire lead-based glazes that were used in eastern Europe at the time, said Parsons. He probably used the technique of grinding up glass and adding salvaged lead to lower the melting point. "Lead is a flux—it acts in a glaze to lower the temperature at which the glass will melt. All glazes are made up of 1) glass, 2) flux (lowers melting temperature) and 3) clay (sticks the glass to the pot). Therefore I feel he used ground-up glass, lead and his local clay for his glazes," said Parsons. "The local clay has minerals and oxides in it. These would affect the colour of the glaze. (e.g. small amounts of iron in the clay can make a yellow, tan or brown glaze. Large amounts of iron make dark brown glazes.) If he wanted a green glaze he only needed to let some copper come in contact with moisture and the blue-green powder resulting (copper oxide) could be added to his glaze for green. Rust (iron oxide) is readily available around old machinery. Cobalt oxide is used to colour glass blue and glazes blue, so he probably ground blue glass for blue."

Kanigan's findings state: "The clustering of the glaze colours into two areas [Yellow, Green-Yellow and Blue-Green] suggest, that although Peter Rupchan had a fairly wide range of colours to chose from, at times his choices may have been limited. The higher amount of combination greens further supports the use of copper as a glaze component. At times the colour of Peter Rupchan's glazes were very mixed and did not present anyone dominant or solid colour" (page 61). Kanigan's concluding findings indicate that, "Peter Rupchan, although capable of expressing a wide range of decorative design, rarely chose to do so..." (page 71) and "...market factors had some bearing upon the way in which he chose to manufacture certain items" (page 74).

"Peter Rupchan utilized a variety of means to decorate his pottery. Aside from completely glazing a vessel, he used glaze as a medium to draw designs on the vessel's surface.... Surface manipulated decorations include incisions...cog-dragged or cog-scribbled lines...or impressions" (page 56).

"Peter Rupchan used a variety of designs when applying glazes. These include; application on only part of the sherd, horizontal straight and wavy lines, vertical lines, circular spots of glaze (either filled in or hollow), splats of glaze and covering a sherd with two distinct colours. He also created a background of solid glaze upon which he painted a design" (page 62).

Use of lead, as flux, in his glazes was another problem. Kanigan found tentative support for "the idea that Rupchan used lead from batteries, at least in the green glaze colours, when mixing his glazes" (page 65-66). "The glaze colours that revealed the highest lead concentrations were green; also the most predominant glaze colour in the sample. Lead is highly toxic, building up in the body over a period of many years. When acidic foods are placed in a lead-glazed vessel the lead is leached out. This process is even more dramatic if the glaze is poorly fired. It is difficult to know if Peter Rupchan was aware of the problems concerning lead poisoning, but many of his vessels, especially crocks used to hold sauerkraut, could have been highly toxic" (page 75). According to Norman Harris's findings, Rupchan's use of lead glaze inside the pots wasn't that common. He would use a glass or silica glaze inside the crocks. Makitras were commonly unglazed. Lead glaze if under-fired would be a problem, but it is doubtful that he used much inside his pots.

In a discussion of the 19 pieces of pottery located in the Ukrainian Museum in Saskatoon, Joan Kanigan in her thesis states on page 29: "All of these pots are attributed to Rupchan, but this can not be verified unequivocally. The vessels were initially authenticated by John Rupchan and John Chalke, an Alberta studio potter, but even they expressed difficulty in identifying certain vessels. It is especially interesting to note that one pot bears a stamp, which are not Peter Rupchan's initials (SE). I have also been told Peter Rupchan never signed his vessels. The problem of identification is further realized because the Ukrainian museum has one crock similar to the ones pulled from Rupchan's kiln. This vessel was never considered to be made by him."

Although it is difficult to determine if some of the pottery pieces reported to be made by Rupchan ever will be definitely authenticated, especially without more extensive testing, there is little doubt that he created a significant amount of pottery that is still in existence. We have to thank the considerate responses of those individuals and organizations that had the prudence and wisdom to see his pottery as the treasure to our heritage that it is. With the dedication and enthusiasm of these people we now come to realize that Rupchan was somewhat of a genius in his own time, working his clay with a passion, fulfilling a dream and leaving behind a meaningful legacy.

Twelve vessel forms were identified from the information gathered...they are: bowls, pots, crocks, flower pots, bottles, cups, whistles, lids and knobs, jars, plates, candlesticks, and dolls." In a condensed version taken from Kanigan's thesis (pages 33-46) there follows a description of each.

Bowls: makitra, flatware (like soup bowls with wide flaring rims), large (mixing) bowls (without cog-dragged impressions on their interior surfaces), small bowls (soup bowls without the wide flaring rim), and straight-rimmed bowls (for lack of a better descriptive word—similar to soup bowls except for the distinct thickening of the rim which is directly in line with the vessel body and is mainly a continuation of the vessel's walls). "Makitras are large bowls which were used to grind seeds such as poppy seed or small amounts of grain...the cog-dragged impressions...on the interior surface...roughen the surface and facilitate grinding seeds.

Crocks: straight-walled cylindrical vessels consructed in a mould in varying sizes, mostly decorated with an overall glaze.

Cooking Pots: open vessels simple in form, similar to bowls and a number of them have handles, used mainly for cooking while bowls tend to be used for food preparation, storage and eating utensils. He made tall-squarish and short-roundish pots (most common). Usually these pots had lids of some type.

Plates: plates, flower pot holders, and flat plates. Utensil plates are eating utensils with a base diameter between 14 and 22 cm. Flower pot holders are smaller, used under flower pots and their base diameter is less than 13 cm. Flat wall-less platter—purpose of these vessels unknown.

Flower Pots: used for decorative purposes—larger vessels for holding numerous or large plants and the smaller more decorated variety. Three rim forms—collared rim, untapered rims and rippled rims.

Cups: an open vessel with a single handle and no spout—rim diameters about 8 cm and base diameters range from 5 cm to 8 cm.

Jars: jugs, pitchers, etc..."having multiple handles and no spout or having no handles nor spout." Jugs are numerous—8 in the Ukrainian Museum of Canada. The average height is about 25 cm.

Handles: three types—strap handles, tube handles and lug handles all made by hand.

Bottles: closed vessels used to hold a variety of liquids—only three sherds available.

Whistles: were made in the form of animals as toys for children. The body is rounded, with a small hole in one side. The mouth piece has a small squarish hole at the top and a larger more rectangular one on the side. The whistles were filled with water to create a warbled whistling noise.

Appendix 3

GLOSSARY OF NAMES

1. In Ukrainian Peter is Petro. He was also sometimes referred to as Pete.

The name "Rupchan" could be spelled Ropchan, Robzcan or Robchan. Robchan, which is the spelling variation that Nikolai used on all his documents, is the Ukrainian version and means labourer or worker. (Rob is the archaic version meaning labourer, robyty means to work) Rupchan is either of Romanian or Ukrainian origins according to the sources below:

a) Professor Yuri Kozholianko, Head of the Department of History and Ethnology at the University of Chernivitsi, in Ukraine, stated his findings:

The community of Molodia is predominantly populated with people of Roumanian descent. Furthermore it was the site of an old German colony (during the period of Austro-Hungarian rule). The name Rupchan appears to have been historically Ropchan. Ropchan, as attested by the residents of Molodia, is of Roumainian origin.

b) The Canadian Institute of Ukrainian Studies said the name Rupchan had no Ukrainian meaning, but that it could possibly be a place name, such as a man from RUP.

c) Norman Harris, a respected historian from the Endeavour area believes the name Rupchan has Slavic (Ukrainian) origins for the following reasons:

i). The area was originally the homeland of Slavic tribes.

ii). The language of culture and administration at the time when family names became mandatory was Ukrainian.

iii). There are other Ukrainian family names with the similar "an" ending, i.e. Chernowchan, Bilan, Galan, Lesan, Toffan.

Harris also states Rupchan can be a place name or name of a noble family that had been changed or shortened over the years. However, if one uses his imagination one can also come up with plausible explanations. At times in Ukraine people lived in sod shanties not unlike the ones found on the prairies during pioneer times. The Ukrainian name for them was Burday or Buda for short. A town to the south of where Peter was born is called Veleka Buda (Big Buda). A name for a root cellar is Rupa; Rupchan can mean a person who lived in a root cellar.

Rupchan could also just mean a slave of a Khan. Rab in Ukrainian was a slave or a worker. Through generations and various ethnic rulers—Maldavian/Turk/Austrain—the pronunciation of Rup and Chan could have been Rab and Khan. Nickoli spelled his name "Robczan", while Pete was "Rupchan."

iv) According to the family Nikolai Rupchan was Romanian, and this is the language he spoke. Peter could speak both, but usually the children recall Ukrainian being spoken in the home. Their mother (Safta) was definitely Ukrainian, as was Peter's mother, who's maiden name was Vihnan.

v) Since Robchan was also used by Nikolai in some of his documents this suggest that he may have changed his name from Robchan to Rupchan for some reason. Note also that his father was Georgii Robchan.

SPELLING VARIATIONS:

Nikolai (Nikolais, Nickolais, Nikolaij), anglicized to Nick (Robchan, Rupchan, Robczan, Ropchan). His parents were Georgii Robchan and Nastasiya Babiak.

Akseniya (Oxenia or Xenia) Vignan, also sometimes spelled Vehnan or Vihnan is a Ukrainian name that means displaced person, wanderer or in exile. It was anglicized to Agnes Wihnan. (The use of "g" was common in Galicia and Bukovina which was part or under the control of Poland.) She was the daughter of Havriel Vihnan and Anna Romanyuk. There were a number of different spellings of personal and location names. H's were sometimes g's and ch's became cz's. As well some towns or villages had at least two spellings—one for Ukrainian and another for the Polish or Austrian authorities.

PLACE NAMES:

Ukrainian: Ruthenian is used to denote people from Bukovina not necessarily all Ukraine. The government of the Russian Empire as well as the Austro-Hungarian Empire outlawed the use of the word Ukrainian. Instead they used the terms Ruthenians or Russene (pronounced Roossenne). The Russians used the words "little Russians" to denote Ukrainians. During the time of the Kingdom of Russ (Roos) people were still in tribal groups, during the Cossack times people already were being referred to as Ukrainian. Ukrainian came into common use after W.W.I. It usually meant people from the Western Ukrainian provinces such as Bukovina, Galicia and Carpatho-Ukraine. It is grammatically incorrect to use "the" before the name of the country Ukraine.

Molodia: It was a village spread along the Derelui River. First mention of the town of Molodia is in the 15th Century. In the area are the remains (traces) of the Trippelian culture 3rd century B.C., early iron mines 1st century A.D. and early Ukrainian settlements 12-13th century. In 1965 there were 3024 people living in Molodia.

Samples of Rupchan's pottery in private collection.

Appendix 4

OTHER POTTERS AND CLAY FACTORIES IN THE PROVINCE

AT APPROXIMATELY THE SAME TIME AS RUPCHAN BEGAN his pottery industry, or even as early as 1902, a potter by the name of Nick Sarota from the Vonda, Saskatchewan area was in operation. The chief colouring of his glazes was reddish brown, as opposed to the green characteristics of Rupchan. Steve Bugera was another Ukrainian potter who migrated to Benito, Manitoba, then moved across the border to Aaran, Saskatchewan. Little is known about his work. It seems Peter Rupchan was the only potter to travel with his wares.

Taken from letters of James Cameron Worcester the following information was derived:

a) In 1912 in Calgary Professor W. G. Worcester was in the process of designing, building and managing the largest face-brick plant in Canada. He was forced to close it down in 1914. By 1921 Worcester, who was considered Canada's foremost authority on ceramics, opened a college of ceramic engineering at the University of Saskatchewan in Saskatoon. Besides being a one man operation it was the first in Canada and the first in the British Commonwealth.

b) "Mr. William Phipps came to the ceramic department when it first opened. He was an assistant, a Yorkshire man who had apprenticed in one of the huge potteries in England; he became a master pottery mold maker. (He came to Calgary from England in 1912, where he worked for Worcester at the face-brick plant.) The ceramic department had a variable speed potters' wheel and Mr. Phipps, Bill as everyone called him, found he had a real talent for the art of turning on a potter's wheel. In ensuing years he was to become the most talented man in the west when it came to the potter's-wheel. I should point out the wheel was only used in the department to demonstrate to visitors the art of hand-turned pottery, of course it could not be sold, but from time to time pieces were given to visiting dignitaries and I am sure examples of his beautiful hand-turned pottery may still be found in some homes not only in Canada but elsewhere. I can say without fear of contradiction Bill Phipps excelled all others of his time when it came to turning on the wheel. He was a Master and a real artist."

c) "A Mrs. Barnett (from Saskatoon) taught clay sculpture in her home in the 1920s."

d) "I [James Cameron Worcester] owned an art pottery in the 1930s and at the same time taught clay modelling and turning on potter's wheels, this was done at the Technical School in Saskatoon. I made all my own glazes, I did the glazing and fusing. I specialized in hand-turned pottery."

The Saskatoon Arts and Crafts Society was a women's group largely in operation during the depression which fostered homecraft. Mrs. Rose Dragan was an important member and organizer of the club that dates from 1923 into the '50s.

1925—The International Clay Products Ltd. took over the plants of the Estevan Brick & Coal Co. Ltd.

Samples of Rupchan's pottery at a Saskatoon Arts and Crafts Society display.

1933—During the year the following plants were in operation: The Bruno Clay Works Ltd., The Dominion Fire Brick & Clay Products Ltd., The International Clay Products Ltd., The Shard Brick & Coal Ltd, and the brick plant at Prince Albert owned by the International Clay Products.

1936—A new firm, Western Paint & Tile Co. Ltd., was launched at Regina. The Canadian Clay Craft, a small art pottery was started at Saskatoon.

1939—The Canadian Clay Craft closed for the duration of the war.

In the 1950s, as a project of the Saskatchewan Arts Board, the Canadian Clay Craft Shop was re-opened. It was acquired in 1961 by Folmer Hansen and David Ross.

BIBLIOGRAPHY

Boychuck, George, son-in-law of Peter Rupchan; "Interviews, and photos."

Boily, Lisi & Blanchette, Jean-Francois, "The Bread Ovens of Quebec," National Museum of Canada, 1979.

"Canora Advertiser," 1912-1919.

Dennis, Landt, "Catch the Wind", Four Winds Press; A Division of Scholastic Magazines, Inc. New York, N.Y., 1976-1974

Department of Arts and Multiculturalism, Government of Saskatchewan, "Correspondence held between themselves and the Ukrainian Museum of Canada, Saskatoon and The Susan Whitney Gallery ."

Dietrich, Zach and Parsons, Wendy, Professional Saskatchewan Potters from Moose Jaw; "Conversations, correspondence and testing of clay."

Harras, Tony Dr., "Letters and interviews of research done on Rupchan's life."

Harris, Norman, from Endeavour, Saskatchewan; "Interviews and notes he collected about the area, people, Rupchan and Ukrainian history," 1980-1990. "Taped and oral interviews with him," 1989-91.

Inch, Mark, "Prairie Wool," *The Western Producer,* 1970.

Kanigan, Joan, Anthropology Department, University of Regina, "Letters, research, and thesis," 1989-90.

Kozholianko, Professor Yuri K., Head of History and Ethnology, University of Chernivitsi, Ukrainian S.S.R., USSR; "Research done on the Rupchan family."

Kudeba, John, from Canora, Saskatchewan, "Oral interviews."

Land Titles, Yorkton, Saskatchewan; "Grants and Certificates of Title."

Lubiniecki, Leo J., "Usherviile Potter Makes Magic with Bits of Clay," The Regina *Leader-Post*, June 24,1939; p.3.

Lubiniecki, Leo J., A Saskatchewan Potter," *The Preeceville Progress,* Nov. 15, 1939.

Lysenko, Vera, "Men in Sheepskin Coats", Ryerson Press, Toronto, 1947.

Main State Archives, Department of Documents and Publications, City of Kiev, Ukrainian S.S.R., U.S.S.R., Birth and marriage certificates.

Martinosky, Lad, "Early Pottery in Saskatchewan," *The Western Producer,* Feb. 19, 1970, C6.

"Past Endeavours: A History of Bear, Beaver Bank, Cheremosz, Endeavour, Lilian, Lilian Rural, Midland, Peerless, Rockford, Stoney Acre, Usherville, Veterans", 1989, Freisen Publishers.

Prestayko, Mrs. Katherine, daughter of Peter Rupchan; "Oral interviews, photograph."

The Regina Leader-Post, June 24, 1939, page 3, article by Lubiniecki, Leo J.

Romanow, Roy, MLA, NDP, Leader of the Opposition (1990), Attorney General and Minister of Culture and Youth (Previously); "Speech given Saturday, January 17, 1981 at the presentation of Rupchan's pottery collection to the Ukrainian Museum."

Ronaghen, Allen Dr., "Kelsey's Journal of 1691 Reconsidered," printed in "Saskatchewan History", Volume xxxvii, No 1, Winter 1984, by the Saskatchewan Archives Board.

Rupchan, George, son of Peter Rupchan: "Taped and oral interviews and photographs."

Rupchan, John, son of Peter Rupchan: "Taped and oral interviews and photographs."

Pettigrew, Eileen, "The Silent Enemy: Canada and the Deadly Flu of 1918," Western Producer Prairie Books. 1983.

Rupchan, Nick, oldest son of Peter Rupchan: "Taped and oral interviews and photographs."

Saskatchewan Archives, Regina and Saskatoon; "Homestead Papers, Maps, Photographs, Correspondence."

Symonds, Richard and Jean, (Symco distributors, Surrey, B.C., 1974) 55 illus. "Medalta Stoneware and pottery for collectors."

Times Books, Ltd., "The Times Historical Atlas," 1978.

Ukrainian Museum of Canada, Saskatoon, Saskatchewan; "Files, artifacts, tapes and photos."

Vital Statistics, Department of, Saskatchewan, "Marriage and death certificates."

Vital Statistics, Administration and Finances, Family Services, Winnipeg, Manitoba, "Death certificate."

The Western Producer, Photo and Caption on the cover of the second section," Feb. 5, 1981.

Worcester, James Cameron, of Sicamous, B.C., "Letters, 1989."

About the Author

J UDITH SILVERTHORNE spent her early years on a farm
in the Glenavon district of Saskatchewan then moved
to Regina in 1959 where she completed her schooling.
Besides being keenly interested in research and history
she enjoys writing about people, past and present. She has
completed three family histories and helped with several
more. Over 300 of her articles have appeared in print in
such publications as "Folklore," "Liaison," "Western People,"
"Western Producer", and "Gardens West," as well as numerous weekly and daily newspapers.

For seven years Judith lived in the Endeavour-
Usherville area of Saskatchewan where Peter Rupchan, the
subject of her book, made his home. While writing an article on Mr. Rupchan she became fascinated by the life he led
and she spent the next three years researching and writing
this book.

Judith Silverthorne currently lives in Regina with her
husband and son. She works as a freelance writer, photog-
rapher and researcher.